T0014652

100 IMMIGRANTS

WHO SHAPED AMERICAN HISTORY

JOANNE MATTERN

sourcebooks
eXplore

Copyright © 2023 by Sourcebooks
Text by Joanne Mattern
Cover design by Will Riley
Illustrations by Westchester Publishing Services
Cover and internal design © 2023 by Sourcebooks

Published by Sourcebooks eXplore, an imprint of Sourcebooks Kids
P.O. Box 4410, Naperville, Illinois 60567-4410
(630) 961-3900
sourcebookskids.com

Cataloging-in-Publication Data is on file with the Library of Congress.

Source of Production: Versa Press, East Peoria, Illinois, USA
Date of Production: August 2023
Trade Paperback ISBN: 9781728290140 Run Number: 5033351
Hardcover ISBN: 9781728290157 Run Number: 5033350

Printed and bound in the United States of America.
VP 10 9 8 7 6 5 4 3 2 1

CONTENTS

Timeline of Birthdates

1760   1855

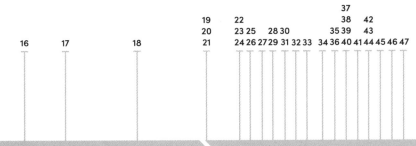

Timeline of Birthdates

1855

1903

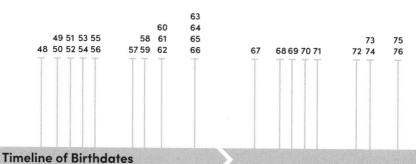

Timeline of Birthdates

1903

1940

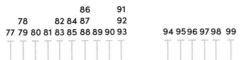

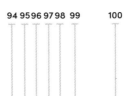

Timeline of Birthdates

1940

2000

INTRODUCTION

THE HISTORY of America has always been guided by the actions and accomplishments of its people. It has been home to countless brilliant thinkers and inventors, great entertainers and writers, and determined activists and changemakers. Many of these great figures were immigrants—people who left the country of their birth to live in the United States.

Immigrants have had a strong presence in the country since its founding. Many around the world saw America as a land that promised new opportunity and endless possibility. In fact, it was not uncommon for immigrants to use the last of their resources to pay their way to America, arriving in their new home penniless and hoping to find their fortune. People like John Jacob Astor, Andrew Carnegie, and Levi Strauss arrived in America with next to nothing, but through hard work and determination, went on to build huge fortunes and establish themselves as icons of American business.

Many inventions and technological developments that helped modernize life in America were pioneered by immigrants. Alexander Graham Bell, Nikola Tesla, Hedy Lamarr, An Wang, and Bjarne Stroustrup all thought up new concepts that would go on to improve the lives of people all over the world. Even one of America's most popular sports was invented by an immigrant, James Naismith.

Immigrants have been central in shaping popular culture in the United States as well. From influential directors like Alfred Hitchcock, Elia Kazan, Lee Strasberg, and M. Night Shyamalan to iconic actors like Bela Lugosi, Great Garbo, Charlie Chaplin, and Anthony Quinn, immigrants have long played a part in creating enduring entertainment for the world as well as catapulting Hollywood into becoming the dominant player in the global film industry. Musicians like Irving Berlin, Itzhak Perlman, and Yo-Yo Ma and artists like Louise Nevelson, Claes Oldenburg, and I. M. Pei have made the cultural history of the United States richer and more diverse.

What people eat in America has also been greatly influenced by immigrants. Individuals like Ettore Boiardi and Joyce Chen dedicated themselves to sharing dishes and recipes from their birth countries with the wider public, making foreign-inspired cuisine accessible to all Americans and introducing new staple dishes into American mealtimes.

Some immigrants leave their home countries seeking better educational and professional opportunities in America. Others simply have few other choices.

Many have had to seek refuge in the United States after being driven out of their home countries due to war or persecution. People like Helena Rubinstein, Hannah Arendt, Isabel Allende, and Ilhan Omar all ended up in America after fleeing dangerous situations in their countries of origin. Activists like Rose Pesotta, Mabel Ping-Hua Lee, Kwame Ture, and Dith Pran used their perspectives to effect change and create a fairer world for everyone.

Together, the one hundred inspiring immigrants in this book represent countless others who have played a major part in shaping America—and who remain an invaluable part of American society today.

JOHN JACOB ASTOR rose from the humblest beginnings to become one of the richest and most important men in America.

Astor was born in the small town of Waldorf, Germany, in 1763, one of twelve children of a poor father who was a farmer and a butcher. Astor was an ambitious young man who wanted a better life than the one available to him in his native land. As a sixteen-year-old young man, he moved to London to work for his older brother, and then in 1783, when he was twenty, Astor traveled to America.

He arrived nearly penniless, but he settled in New York City and worked at various jobs before becoming a clerk to a **fur trader**. Astor quickly learned the fur-trading business and his employer soon had him completing deals in London. Around this time, Astor also met and married a young woman named Sarah Todd. They had eight children, five of whom survived to adulthood.

By 1786, Astor had entered the fur trade on his own. He had a lot of business sense and was willing to work hard, and within six years, he had become very wealthy buying and selling furs.

In 1808, Astor formed the **American Fur Company** to take advantage of newly acquired land from the Louisiana Purchase. In 1810, he formed the **Pacific Fur Company** subsidiary, and the following year, he established a trading post at the mouth of the Columbia River in the Oregon Territory (present-day Oregon), naming it **Astoria**.

Soon Astor had a monopoly on fur trade in America. Although the market for furs in the United States was strong, Astor knew he could make even more money overseas. He bought his own fleet of ships and used them to transport furs to China. On the return trip, these ships carried manufactured goods and teas that Astor would sell in America and Europe. These ventures made Astor the first multimillionaire in the United States.

While he was accumulating his wealth, Astor began to invest in real estate, especially in New York City. He purchased cheap land north of the city's developed area and then waited until the city grew enough and needed to develop his lots. It was a brilliant strategy, and it secured intergenerational wealth for Astor and his heirs.

In 1834, Astor left the fur-trading business and devoted the rest of his life to managing his real estate holdings. He also donated $400,000 to establish the **Astor Library**, which would eventually merge with two other institutions to become the great New York Public Library.

When Astor died, he left the bulk of his personal fortune of more than $20 million to his son, William Backhouse Astor, who went on to double the family's real estate holdings to nearly $50 million. Many of Astor's descendants went on to become influential in their own right.

SAMUEL SLATER was blessed with a brilliant mind and a photographic memory. When he used both to transport the knowledge he acquired at home in England to the United States, it led to the development of the American factory system and earned him the name **"Founder of the American Industrial Revolution."**

Slater was born in 1768 in Derbyshire, England, the son of a successful farmer and landowner. When Slater was young, a man named Jedediah Strutt bought the rights to use land and water that belonged to Slater's father. Strutt's partner, Richard Arkwright, had developed a system to card and spin cotton, and Arkwright wanted to build a **textile mill** on Slater's land. As part of the business deal, Strutt and Arkwright offered to train one of Slater's sons in textiles. Fourteen-year-old Sam was chosen because he was organized and very good at arithmetic.

For seven years, the young man worked as Strutt's apprentice and learned every part of the textile business. By the time his apprenticeship ended in 1789, Slater felt that the textile industry in England had reached its peak. He thought that he could do better if he took his knowledge to the fledgling nation across the Atlantic Ocean—the United States.

However, at that time the British government did not allow skilled mechanics to emigrate because they did not want to share the country's technical knowledge. To leave England, Slater dressed simply and told everyone he was a farm laborer. Using this disguise, he was able to board a British ship and sail to New York City. No one knew that he had memorized complicated machine specifications and mechanical plans.

Soon after arriving, Slater went to Pawtucket, Rhode Island, to work with Moses Brown, an American merchant who wanted to start a factory based on Richard Arkwright's system. Slater rebuilt Brown's old machines, and by 1792, the mill was very successful. In 1793, Slater built his own mill in Pawtucket. Slater Mill became the first successful water-powered textile mill in the city, and he went on to own many textile mills in the area.

Slater enlisted entire families, including children, to work in his mills. These families lived in company-owned housing and attended company-run schools and churches. Slater's system soon became the model for many factories and led to the development of **mill towns** throughout New England. Although New England's textile mills would later be shamed for their exploitation of women and children for labor, in Slater's time, they were considered decent places to work.

Slater married twice and had nine children. When he died in 1835, he was worth more than $1.2 million, a tremendous amount of money in those times. His innovations helped change the United States from an agricultural economy to an industrial one.

The name Audubon is synonymous with **birds and bird-watching**. This is a fitting legacy for a man who, as a self-taught **naturalist** and artist, introduced the great variety of American birds to the world.

JOHN JAMES AUDUBON was born in Saint-Domingue in the West Indies (present-day Haiti) on April 26, 1785, to a French sea captain and a Creole woman. Audubon lived

there until he was four years old. After being adopted legally by his father, he was then sent to Nantes, France, to be raised by his father's wife. Audubon received an excellent education, and in his studies, he was especially interested in nature, drawing, and music.

When Audubon was eighteen, his family sent him to live with relatives in Pennsylvania to avoid being drafted into Napoleon's army. Audubon spent his time there studying nature and drawing birds. He also met and married a woman named Lucy Bakewell.

Despite his interest in birds, Audubon made his living doing business. He eventually moved to western Kentucky, where he ran a dry goods store on the frontier. While in Kentucky, Lucy gave birth to two sons and a daughter, who died in infancy.

In 1819, after Audubon's business failed, he decided the time was right to devote himself to his first love—drawing birds. Taking along his art materials and an assistant, Audubon set off down the Mississippi River. He also explored the Ohio River Valley and the Great Lakes region, drawing every bird he saw.

In 1826, Audubon tried to find an American publisher for his drawings, but no one was interested. Instead, he traveled to England, showed his work to publishers there, and found much more enthusiasm. His subsequent four-volume work, **The Birds of America**, immediately became a huge success. People all over Europe admired his life-size, full-bodied, and dramatic bird portraits accompanied by his descriptions of wildlife.

In 1831, Audubon returned to the United States as a wealthy and famous man. In 1938, he published a smaller version of *The Birds of America,* thus exposing his work to an even wider audience.

Audubon settled in New York City, but in 1843, he made another trip west to observe mammals. When he returned home, he brought with him a collection of live deer, foxes, and badgers to use as models for his last book, *The Viviparous Quadrupeds of North America.* However, Audubon fell ill and was unable to complete the book. The art was largely completed by his sons, and the text was written by a friend.

Audubon died on January 27, 1851. Later, when a group of bird lovers decided to start a society focused on bird conservation, they asked Audubon's widow for permission to use his name. She agreed, and the **National Audubon Society** lives on today, carrying on their namesake's love of birds and nature.

Today, **suspension bridges** soar majestically over waterways in many American cities. However, up until the late nineteenth century, this type of bridge was unheard of. It took an immigrant from Germany to show the world how to build these mighty structures.

JOHN AUGUSTUS ROEBLING was born on June 12, 1806, in Mühlhausen, Prussia (present-day Germany). As a young man, he attended the Royal Polytechnic School in Berlin, Germany, where his courses included engineering, architecture, and bridge construction. Roebling graduated in 1826 and spent the next three years building roads as part of his required military service.

Roebling dreamed of being a farmer, and in 1831, he came to the United States. He purchased land outside Pittsburgh, Pennsylvania, where he established a farm and built a town called Saxonburg. However, Roebling soon got bored with farming and decided to return to engineering work. When he heard that the Pennsylvania Railroad Corporation was looking for a surveyor, Roebling took the job. He also worked as an engineer for the state of Pennsylvania, helping to locate and map routes for railroads and canals.

In 1841, Roebling invented a twisted wire rope cable that could support heavy loads over a long distance. In 1844, he put his wire to use when he was awarded the job of building a bridge over the Allegheny River. Roebling had only nine months to complete the job, but in that short time, he built the first suspension bridge. Other engineers ridiculed Roebling's bridge and said that the water rushing around the structure would knock it down. Roebling knew they were wrong, and the bridge remained standing.

Roebling built several more bridges in Pennsylvania over the next few years. In 1847, he established a factory in New Jersey to manufacture his wire cable. He also built railroad bridges over the Niagara and Ohio rivers.

However, Roebling's most famous job was designing and constructing the **Brooklyn Bridge** in New York City. He began work on the bridge in 1867, but the project was cut short on July 6, 1869. Roebling was standing on a ferry slip when a boat smashed into the dock and crushed one of his feet. The injury became infected, and Roebling died sixteen days later on July 22.

Construction on the bridge continued under the direction of Roebling's son, Washington Augustus. In 1872, misfortune struck again when the younger Roebling became permanently disabled by decompression sickness after he entered an underwater chamber called a caisson. However, he continued working, assisted by his wife, Emily Warren Roebling, and managed to complete the bridge in 1883.

When the Brooklyn Bridge opened to the public, it was the longest bridge in the world, spanning 1,595 feet over the East River, connecting Manhattan and Brooklyn. The bridge remains a busy and popular site today, and it stands as a fitting monument to John Augustus Roebling's mechanical genius.

Of the thousands of **saints** canonized by the Roman Catholic church, only a few have come from America. The first male saint from the United States actually was born in Europe, but he went on to do great works in his adopted home.

JOHN NEPOMUCENE NEUMANN was born on March 28, 1811, in Bohemia (present-day Czech Republic). From childhood, he dreamed of becoming a priest, and he went on to complete his theological studies at the University of Prague. During his education, Neumann learned several languages, and this skill proved very useful when he came to the United States.

In 1836, Neumann arrived in New York City, where he was ordained in June of that year. Then the young priest was sent to work in a parish in Buffalo, New York, which at the time was a very rural area populated with many European immigrants. Later, Neumann worked in several parishes in Pennsylvania, which also had many German and Irish immigrants who had come to work in the coal mines.

Father Neumann built churches and schools in this area and taught children himself. He learned Irish dialects so that he could hear confessions from Irish immigrants who could not speak English. By the late 1840s, he was serving in Baltimore, Maryland, and in 1848, he became a U.S. citizen.

In 1852, Neumann was named the bishop of Philadelphia. That city was filled with many different immigrant groups, and Neumann set out to help all of them. Italians especially loved him. Italian immigrants in Philadelphia had no priest who spoke their language, so they felt very isolated. Neumann had learned Italian during his theological studies, and he invited the city's Italian community to come to his private chapel to hear Mass. In 1855, he purchased a Methodist church and dedicated it to **St. Mary Magdalene de Pazzi**. At last, Philadelphia's Italians had a church of their own.

Neumann also understood the value of a Catholic education. In May 1852, he created the first unified system of **Catholic schools** under the direction of a diocese. This system is still used today throughout the United States. Speaking of Neumann's work, Pope Pius XII later said, "It was mainly through his prodigious efforts that a Catholic school system came into being and that parochial schools began to rise across the land."

Neumann continued working until he died suddenly of a heart attack on January 5, 1860. After his death, thousands came to his church to honor him. Stories of miracles Neumann had performed also began to spread. Efforts began to name him a saint. Finally, after many years of investigation and research, Neumann became **St. John Neumann** in 1977. Today, pilgrims continue to travel to Philadelphia to honor Neumann.

Some immigrants came to the United States to escape a troubled past. Once in America, however, they turned their energy to more productive uses, and helped shape the future of the country.

THOMAS FRANCIS MEAGHER was born in Waterford, Ireland, on August 3, 1823. When he was just eleven years old, he went to live with a group of Jesuit priests in County Kildare. He did well in school there, and the Jesuits later sent him to Stonyhurst College in England, where he studied classic literature, mathematics, and history. Meagher graduated from Stonyhurst and returned to Ireland in 1843.

At that time, Ireland was fighting against British rule, and Meagher became a leader in the movement to gain **Irish independence**. Due to his activities, he and eight other men were arrested and sentenced to death by hanging in 1848. However, England's Queen Victoria lessened the sentence in response to public outcry. Instead of executing him, the government exiled Meagher to Australia.

Meagher arrived in Australia in 1849, and like many British transports, he was able to live a normal life. He married the daughter of another Irish rebel and had a son. Although he was free, life was hard, and Meagher dreamed of better things.

In 1852, Meagher left Australia without permission and traveled to the United States. Settling in New York City, he became a popular public speaker, author, and lawyer. Meagher's wife remained behind and died in 1854. The next year, he married Elizabeth Townsend, the daughter of a prominent New York family.

In 1861, the **American Civil War** began. Meagher was a die-hard supporter of the Union, and he organized a company of New York soldiers that became known as the Irish Brigade. Meagher's courage and leadership qualities quickly led to his appointment as a brigadier general.

Meagher fought in such famous battles as Bull Run, Antietam, Chancellorsville, and Gettysburg. His support for the Union never wavered, even when many people doubted that the United States could ever be restored as one nation. Meagher once wrote of the Union cause, "Never was there a cause more sacred, nor one more great, nor one more urgent."

By the time the American Civil War ended in 1865, Meagher was a **military hero**. As a reward for his service, the U.S. government appointed him the acting governor of Montana, which was then a territory. As part of his responsibilities, Meagher faced conflicts with American Indians and other dangers of the frontier.

On July 5, 1867, Meagher was on a steamboat on the Missouri River when he tripped over some rope and fell into the river. His body was swept away by the swift current and was never found. In his relatively short life, Thomas Meagher contributed greatly to his adopted land.

During the 1850s, "**gold fever**" gripped Americans as thousands flocked to the western reaches of the country hoping to find gold and strike it rich. Most of these prospectors had no success, but one German immigrant became wealthy thanks to the Gold Rush by capitalizing on what every person, rich or poor, uses—**clothing**.

LEVI STRAUSS was born on February 26, 1829, in the small village of Buttenheim, Bavaria, which later became part of modern-day Germany. Strauss's father was a **peddler** who went door-to-door selling supplies such as cloth, tools, pots, and sewing needles. He could barely support his seven children and his wife. Life was even more difficult because the Strauss family was Jewish. At that time, Jewish people were treated badly in many places and faced restrictions on where they could live and work.

When Strauss was sixteen, his father died. Strauss took up the peddler's trade, but he longed for a better future. Two of his brothers had emigrated to New York a few years earlier, and in 1847, Strauss, his mother, and two of his sisters joined them.

Strauss went to work at his brothers' dry goods business in New York. In 1853, Strauss became a U.S. citizen, and that same year, he decided to go to California, which, since the discovery of gold in 1849, had been flooded with prospectors looking to get rich. Strauss wanted to open a dry goods store and sell clothes, tools, and supplies to all the gold miners.

In March 1853, Strauss opened a store in San Francisco. He soon developed a reputation as an honest and fair businessperson, and by 1866, he moved to a bigger location and called his business **Levi Strauss & Co**.

In 1872, a tailor named Jacob Davis wrote to Strauss. Davis had developed a way to make pants stronger by sewing on **metal**

rivets to keep them from ripping. Davis wanted to patent his idea, but he didn't have enough money. He asked Strauss for financial help, and in exchange, offered to share the patent with him and allow Strauss to manufacture and sell the pants. Strauss agreed, and it turned out to be the smartest business decision he would ever make.

Strauss could barely keep up with the orders from miners, cowboys, railroad workers, and farmers who wanted the sturdy pants. He became very wealthy, and he donated some of his money to orphanages, schools, and other charities. He never married and said that all his happiness was in his business.

Strauss died on September 26, 1902. Today, "Levis" is synonymous with **jeans**, and Levi Strauss is still one of the biggest jeans manufacturers in the world.

ANDREW CARNEGIE came to America as a poor young boy, amassed a fortune worth hundreds of millions of dollars, and then generously gave much of it away to become the most noted philanthropist in U.S. history.

Carnegie was born in Dunfermline, Scotland, on November 25, 1835. His father was a weaver, but at that time, the weaving trade was in jeopardy because newly developed machines could make cloth more quickly and cheaply. By 1848, Carnegie's father was out of work, and the family was desperate. Twelve-year old Carnegie and his family sailed to America in search of a more promising future, and they settled in Allegheny, Pennsylvania.

Carnegie hated to leave Scotland, but he loved the idea of the **American dream** that anyone could do well, regardless of their background. At first, conditions for the family in America weren't much better than they had been at home. His father could not find work, and his mother had to support the family by making shoes.

Carnegie found a job for two dollars a week at a textile mill. He ran the boiler, dipped cotton in oil, and helped the owner pay bills and write letters. Two years later, Carnegie got a better job delivering messages for a telegraph company in Pittsburgh. Within a few years, he had advanced to telegraph operator, and by the age of twenty-four, he had become the superintendent of the western division of the **Pennsylvania Railroad**.

With the help of a loan and some advice from a top railroad official, Carnegie began to invest in stocks. By the time he reached his thirties, he was very wealthy.

During the 1870s, Carnegie concentrated all his resources into the production of steel. He hired top experts in steel technology and plant management, kept costs low by holding down wages and salaries, and undercut his competitors' prices. Before long, Carnegie had built an empire within the **steel industry**.

When he was fifty-one years old, Carnegie married twenty-three-year-old Louise Whitfield. The couple had one daughter named Margaret.

By the end of the 1800s, Carnegie controlled about 25 percent of the iron and steel production in the United States. In 1901, he sold his company for $480 million and retired as one of the richest people in the world.

Carnegie donated money to charities throughout his life. He was especially interested in providing educational opportunities to the poor. During his lifetime, Carnegie gave more than $350 million to colleges, research institutions, and most significantly, to **libraries**. He paid for the construction of almost three thousand libraries in the United States.

Carnegie died of pneumonia at home in Lenox, Massachusetts, on August 11, 1919. He was eighty-three years old, and he left a legacy that improved the lives of millions.

As a young boy at home in Scotland, **JOHN MUIR** dreamed of one day seeing the **American wilderness**. As an adult living in his adopted country, he was primarily responsible for helping to preserve millions of acres of that very wilderness for future generations to cherish.

John Muir was born in Dunbar, Scotland, on April 21, 1838. From his earliest childhood days, Muir loved nature. The boy was also fascinated by stories of the American wilderness, and he hoped to see it for himself someday.

That day came sooner than Muir had expected. When he was eleven years old, the family moved to a farm in Wisconsin. Although Muir wanted to spend all his time exploring the thick woods, his father insisted that he and his siblings help with the farm work.

When Muir was twenty-two years old, he enrolled at the University of Wisconsin. He studied chemistry and geology among other things, but he left after three years without graduating.

By 1867, Muir decided to begin pursuing his passion—exploring the wilderness, writing about his discoveries, and persuading others to preserve as much of the wilderness as possible. That year, he walked from Indiana to the Gulf of Mexico, and he recorded his observations of **flora and fauna** in a journal.

Years later these observations were published in his book, *A Thousand Mile Walk to the Gulf.* Muir then traveled to the far west and spent six years in the vicinity of the Yosemite Valley in California, a place he grew to love. As Muir continued to travel throughout the west and later to Alaska, he saw firsthand how timber companies, ranchers, and rapid industrialization were destroying the wilderness. He spoke publicly about the need to preserve it, saying, "People need beauty as well as bread."

In 1880, Muir married Louise Strentzel, and they had two daughters. Muir also purchased part of the family's fruit ranch from his father-in-law, and for the next ten years, he turned his interests to horticulture.

Muir's conservation efforts led to laws to protect California's **redwood forests** and other natural treasures, and they also spurred Congress to establish the **Yosemite** and **Sequoia national parks** in 1890. In 1892, Muir also founded the **Sierra Club**, which was devoted to the preservation of the wilderness.

Muir used his friendship with **President Theodore Roosevelt**, another ardent conservationist, to help preserve nature's beauty. In 1903, Muir took Roosevelt hiking in the Yosemite Valley, and before Roosevelt left office in 1908, he had doubled the number of national parks across America, protecting 145 million acres of wilderness.

Muir died at home in California on December 24, 1914. His house is now a national historic site, and a redwood forest in Marin County near San Francisco was named **Muir Woods** in his honor.

When a young immigrant from Scotland tried to determine whether **voice vibrations** could be turned into electrical signals and transmitted through wires, he developed one of the greatest advancements in the history of communications.

ALEXANDER GRAHAM BELL was born in Edinburgh, Scotland, on March 3, 1847. From childhood, Bell was familiar with the world of the hearing impaired—his mother

was deaf, and his father developed a system that used drawings of the mouth, tongue, and lips to teach deaf people how to speak.

Bell attended universities in London and Edinburgh, and then when he was twenty-three, he and his parents moved to Ontario, Canada. The following year, Bell moved to Boston, Massachusetts, and got a job teaching at a school for deaf students, using the system his father developed. Later, Bell married one of his students, Mabel Hubbard. The couple went on to have two daughters, Elsie May and Marion Daisy, and two sons who died in infancy.

In 1873, Bell became a professor of speech and vocal physiology at Boston University. While teaching, Bell began experimenting with a means of transmitting several telegraph messages over a single wire simultaneously, as well as trying various devices to help deaf people learn to speak. He wondered if voice vibrations could be turned into electrical signals and sent through wires.

One day in March 1876, as he was working with his assistant Thomas Watson, Bell spilled some battery acid onto his pants. Bell called out, "Watson, come here. I want you." And although Watson was in another room, he heard Bell's voice come across wires and through a **receiver** connected to a transmitter Bell had designed. Bell's idea worked.

In June 1876, Bell displayed his invention at a huge fair called the Centennial Exposition in Philadelphia. It was the most popular exhibit at the expo, and news of the telephone quickly spread throughout the country.

Other inventors had worked on ideas for the telephone, but Bell was the first to successfully patent his invention. In 1877, with the help of his father-in-law, he founded the **Bell Telephone Company**, the nation's first telephone company.

Bell earned great public acclaim as well as great financial success with his invention. During his lifetime, he also invented several other machines, including an electrical probe to find bullets in the human body.

Bell also donated money to scientific groups to encourage them to develop new inventions. In 1888, he and his father-in-law along with several others founded the **National Geographic Society** to encourage exploration and scientific developments around the world.

He also continued to work extensively on behalf of the deaf community, and in 1890, he founded the **Alexander Graham Bell Association for the Deaf and Hard of Hearing**.

Alexander Graham Bell died on August 2, 1922.

JOSEPH PULITZER, a founding figure of modern **journalism** whose name still represents excellence and outstanding performance, was a man of immense personal drive and work ethic.

Born in Makó, Hungary, on April 10, 1847, to a wealthy Jewish family, Joseph Pulitzer began his lifelong love of education early, eagerly learning from the tutors and schools around Budapest where he was raised. This love served him well, and by the time he was seventeen, Pulitzer was already a well-read and curious young man who spoke both German and French, and who had begun to learn English.

Despite his safe and sheltered upbringing, Pulitzer decided that he wanted to both see the world and serve in the military, attempting to enlist in the Austrian Army, Napoleon's Foreign Legion, and even the British Army. Unfortunately, because of Joseph's poor eyesight and weak health, he was denied entry into all three forces. Determined to serve, however, the young Pulitzer eventually met a recruiter for the U.S. Union Army in Germany, and through a complicated process, was accepted into the Union Forces. During the American Civil War, Joseph Pulitzer served with German cavalry units.

After the Civil War, the young Pulitzer worked his way across America as he headed to St. Louis, earning his passage and making a living as a waiter, baggage handler, and general laborer. During this time, he worked on his knowledge of the English language and of law, studying eagerly at the St. Louis Mercantile Library. It was at this library that Joseph Pulitzer's real career began. After boldly commenting on a chess move between two men playing at the library, the men offered Joseph a job at their newspaper—the **Westliche Post**.

For the next several years, Joseph Pulitzer dedicated himself fiercely to his work, and only four years after being hired to the *Westliche*, he was given the chance to become publisher of the paper. Pulitzer was thrilled at the opportunity, and at only twenty-five years of age, he became one of St. Louis's most promising young journalists. As publisher of the *Westliche Post*, Joseph worked tirelessly to master his craft, and in only a few short years he had become the proud owner of the **St. Louis Post–Dispatch**.

Though Joseph's trademark work ethic brought him great professional success throughout his life, it also cost him his health. Records and firsthand accounts from friends and employees of Pulitzer often said that he routinely worked sixteen-hour days. So hard was this work on Joseph that he was ordered to take a vacation by his doctor, which he refused. Instead, Pulitzer met with fellow business partner Jay Gould and successfully purchased the **New York World**, a well-respected New York paper.

With the *New York World*, Pulitzer worked to make the paper a voice for the common people, using its pages to expose corruption and champion social reform that helped improve the lives of average Americans. His contributions to American journalism were so great that, after his death, the **Pulitzer Prize** organization was founded in his name, dedicated to awarding prizes to outstanding authors who have helped change the world with their work.

The vivid depictions, in photographs and words, of the harsh realities of New York's slums by a Danish immigrant in the late nineteenth century showed the world the hardships of urban immigrant life and helped bring about much needed **social reform**.

JACOB AUGUST RIIS was born in Ribe, Denmark, on May 3, 1849. His father was the town's schoolmaster, and he also wrote for the local newspaper. He struggled to support his large family, which included fifteen children.

Riis dropped out of school when he was fifteen to become an apprentice to a local carpenter. He remained dissatisfied with his life, however, and after a local girl named Elizabeth Nielsen refused to marry him, Riis decided to emigrate to America.

Riis arrived in New York in April 1870, and his first few years in America were very difficult. He struggled to find carpentry work and was often homeless and penniless. Finally, in 1877, he got a job as a police reporter for the *New York Tribune*.

Along with stories about crime, Riis wrote a series of articles about poverty in the city, particularly in the slums where large numbers of immigrants lived. Accompanying the articles were photographs he took, which featured street children, garment workers, and families crowded into unsanitary **tenements**. Riis was one of the first reporters to use **flash photography**, which allowed him to take pictures inside dark apartments, factories, and prisons.

In 1888, Riis went to work for another newspaper, the *Evening Sun*. He also developed his articles into a series of books. His most famous title, **How the Other Half Lives**, was published in 1890. In it, he documented such living conditions as finding five families, totaling twenty people, living in one twelve-by-twelve room and with two beds for them all. Riis found that there were more than forty thousand such tenements in New York City, and none of them had running water or flushable toilets for the more than one million residents.

Riis's work shocked the public and led to reforms in **child labor laws** and improvements in housing and education. Soon, other cities followed New York's example and created better living conditions for their poor immigrants as well.

Riis published his autobiography, *The Making of an American,* in 1901. He continued to write, take photographs, and give public lectures despite developing a heart condition in 1904. He also campaigned and helped raise money to build playgrounds and parks in New York's poor neighborhoods.

Riis's personal life was rewarding as well. Elizabeth, his love in Denmark, had immigrated to the United States, and the couple married in 1876. They had four children and lived happily until Elizabeth's death in 1905. Two years later, Riis married his secretary, Mary A. Phillips.

Riis remained active until he died of heart failure on May 25, 1914.

As a poor child growing up in a grimy English city, **FRANCES HODGSON BURNETT** dreamed of beautiful gardens. She turned her dreams into stories that children all over the world would grow to love and that would make Burnett one of the most famous authors of her time.

Frances Eliza Hodgson was born in Manchester, England, on November 24, 1849, the middle child of five children. Frances always loved to write **stories**, and even though her older brothers teased her, Frances kept on making them up.

Frances's father ran a hardware business. Sadly, he died when Frances was very young, leaving her mother to run the business. By 1865, the family was in serious financial trouble. Mrs. Hodgson's brother wrote to her from Tennessee and invited the family to come live with him in America.

Frances was sixteen years old when she arrived in Tennessee. Although her brothers soon found work in a store, the family remained desperately poor. Frances decided to try to sell some of her stories. By the time she was eighteen, she was **publishing** several stories a month in popular women's magazines of the time, and she had become the breadwinner in her family. Her brothers never teased her about her writing again.

In 1873, Frances married a close friend named Swan Burnett, and the couple had two sons. Frances was never really in love with Swan, although they remained together for a long time. They divorced in 1898.

In addition to her magazine stories, Burnett wrote fifty-five books, mostly for adults. Some of her most popular novels were *That Lass O'Lowrie's*, *A Lady of Quality*, and its sequel, *His Grace of Osmond*.

When her younger son asked her to write a book for boys, Burnett agreed. The book, **Little Lord Fauntleroy**, became the most popular book of its time in 1886. The novel was so popular that many parents dressed their children in fancy suits like those worn by the titular character. In 1936, the book was turned into a popular Hollywood movie.

Following her divorce, Burnett lived for a little while in England. After a man wrote a stage version of *Little Lord Fauntleroy* without her permission, Burnett became active in the fight to create a fairer copyright law for authors.

Although she considered herself British, Burnett also felt American because her two sons were American. In 1905, she became a U.S. citizen, and then moved into a large estate on Long Island, New York. She filled the grounds with gardens and spent most of her time writing. In 1911, Burnett wrote her most enduring children's book there, the classic **The Secret Garden**.

Frances Hodgson Burnett died at her Long Island home on October 29, 1924. Her work has lived on to charm generations of young readers.

SAMUEL GOMPERS endured the harsh realities of a working life from a very young age. As an adult, he became one of the founders of America's **labor movement**.

Gompers was born into a Jewish family in London, England, on January 27, 1850. The family—which included Gompers, his parents, and his four younger brothers—lived in a crowded two-room apartment on the ground floor of a house.

Gompers attended a Jewish school and was an excellent student. However, when he was ten years old, he had to leave school to help support his family. Gompers began rolling cigars, just as his father did.

The family's economic situation became increasingly difficult, and in 1863, they emigrated to New York City in search of more opportunities. They settled into a **tenement** in a Jewish neighborhood in lower Manhattan. Young Gompers continued making cigars until he found a job in a local store. At the age of sixteen, he married Sophia Julian. They went on to have twelve children, and their marriage lasted until her death in 1920.

Gompers joined a local cigar makers' union when he was only fourteen years old. Over the next few years, he met many older labor reformers and became interested in the concept of **trade unions** to bring about social reform.

In 1875, Gompers was elected president of the local chapter of the Cigar Makers' International Union. In 1881, he helped establish the Federation of Organized Trades and Labor Unions. In 1886, the Federation reorganized and took a new name: the **American Federation of Labor** (AFL). Gompers was elected president of the AFL, a post he held until his death thirty-eight years later.

Gompers worked to make the labor movement powerful enough to change the economic, social, and political status of America's trade workers. He advocated trade unionism, meaning that workers would form local unions based on their trade or craft. Gompers also insisted that unions remain politically neutral and only support candidates that agreed with the union's beliefs.

Soon after his election as AFL president, Gompers began building a national federation of trade unions. Over the next twenty-five years, AFL membership soared, and the AFL was able to help elect union members and labor-friendly candidates to political office.

In 1912, the AFL actively supported the successful Democratic presidential candidate, **Woodrow Wilson**. Over the next several years, the AFL and Gompers helped obtain enactment of pro-labor legislation such as the **Clayton Antitrust Act**.

During World War I, President Wilson appointed Gompers to the **Council of National Defense**, where he helped gather labor support for the war. In return, Gompers got the Wilson administration to ensure business leaders would negotiate with union leaders, which guaranteed wartime production and enabled union membership to grow.

Samuel Gompers died in San Antonio, Texas, on December 13, 1924.

As a young **nun** in Italy, **MOTHER CABRINI** dreamed of being a missionary in China. The pope's decision to send her to America to help immigrants there had an enormous beneficial effect on American society and resulted in Cabrini becoming the first U.S. citizen to be **canonized** by the Roman Catholic church.

She was born Maria Francesca Cabrini on July 15, 1850, in the small town of Sant'Angelo Lodigiano, Italy. She was the youngest of thirteen children, and her parents owned a small farm. Young Maria worked hard on the farm alongside her brothers and sisters. She grew up enthralled by stories of missionaries and was determined to become one herself.

After her parents died in 1870, she applied to join her teachers at the Daughters of the Sacred Heart, but they reluctantly refused her, thinking her frail health made her ill-suited for the hard life of a missionary. But in 1874, she was asked to manage an orphanage, and was finally allowed to take her vows in 1877, at which time she changed her name to Frances Xavier Cabrini, in honor of the patron saint of missionaries. In 1880, she and seven other young women formed the **Missionary Sisters of the Sacred Heart**. Their work supported and offered schooling to orphans, and it was during this time that Frances became known as Mother Cabrini.

Cabrini and her sisters planned to go China as missionaries, but Pope Leo XIII reportedly told her to go "not to the East, but to the West"—she was to go to America to minister to the many Italian immigrants there. Cabrini, along with six nuns, arrived in New York City in March 1889. She quickly worked to raise money to build a convent and an orphanage, and she also started a hospital to care for the city's poor immigrants.

Cabrini was not physically strong, but she possessed tremendous determination. She also had a lot of faith in God and believed God would provide whatever she needed. For the next twenty-eight years after her arrival in America, she devoted herself to improving the lives of America's orphans and poor families.

For the next twenty-eight years after her arrival in America, Cabrini traveled around the United States and founded sixty-seven schools, hospitals, and orphanages over the course of her life. In 1909, Mother Cabrini became a U.S. citizen. Most of her work was in New York, Chicago, Seattle, and New Orleans, which were all cities with large immigrant populations. Eventually the Missionary Sisters expanded throughout South America and Europe, founding institutions in Buenos Aires, Paris, Madrid, and Rio de Janeiro, and today their order can be found on six continents across the globe.

Mother Cabrini died eight years later in Chicago, on December 22, 1917. A movement to make Mother Cabrini a saint began shortly after her death. She was finally canonized St. Frances Xavier Cabrini in 1946, and in 1950 she was named Patroness of Immigrants. The story of the woman considered too weak to be a missionary eventually becoming the patron saint of immigrants continues to inspire. In 2020, a statue of Mother Cabrini was unveiled in New York City's Battery Park. The statue overlooks New York Harbor to honor Mother Cabrini's work with immigrants.

NIKOLA TESLA was a legendary scientist, engineer, and inventor whose brilliance has helped shape modern technology. Despite personal and professional struggles, Tesla's genius and unwavering dedication to his work set him apart as one of history's most influential minds.

Born on July 10, 1856, of humble beginnings in Smiljan, Croatia, Nikola Tesla's father was a priest in the Orthodox Church, and his mother ran the farm where their family lived. Though Tesla's early childhood was simple and provincial in many respects, his mother sparked a love of electricity and engineering in him from an early age. As a hobby, he often invented small electrical appliances to help with tasks around the house and farm. Though his father hoped that he would join the priesthood, Nikola's attraction to **invention and technology** was too strong, and as a young man, he eagerly began his formal education in the sciences.

While attending respected institutes in both Germany and Austria, Nikola Tesla quickly established himself as an unusually bright and capable student. After his time at university, Tesla moved to Budapest, Hungary, where he found a job with a telephone company. It was in Budapest that Tesla was struck by an idea for a revolutionary type of **motor** while on a casual stroll. Though Nikola worked tirelessly to win funding for his research and invention, many investors failed to understand the potential impact of the young engineer's work. Still, convinced of his motor's potential, Nikola Tesla decided to move to the United States and continue his research.

In the United States, Tesla quickly met with fellow inventor and entrepreneur **Thomas Edison,** who recognizing the young man's brilliance, hired Tesla almost immediately. For months, the two worked side by side to improve existing electrical technology, with Tesla helping refine and advance many of Edison's inventions. A difference in personalities, however, meant that the duo soon separated. While Edison was a dedicated businessperson whose love of technology was tied to money, Tesla himself was an idealist, who looked to invent new and better technologies purely for the advancement of science and humankind.

After leaving his job with Edison, Nikola Tesla continued his personal work to design and improve electrical devices. Over the next several decades, he went on to invent countless technological innovations such as **radar**, **X-ray machines**, **hydroelectric power plants**, and of course, his famous **Tesla coil**, which is still widely used today.

Today, Tesla is remembered as a genius almost without equal in history, who persevered through personal hardship in order to help revolutionize electrical technology and help shape the modern world. A man of powerful ideals and commitment, Nikola Tesla is truly one of science's greatest legends.

One of America's most popular amateur and professional sports was invented in the late nineteenth century by a young immigrant and theological student looking to combine ministerial work and athletics.

JAMES NAISMITH was born on November 6, 1861, in Almonte, Canada. His parents had immigrated to Canada from Scotland some years earlier, and his father worked in a sawmill. James's childhood was full of heartbreak. Both of his parents died in 1871 during a typhoid fever epidemic. James, his brother, and his sister went to live with their grandmother. When she died just two years later, an uncle named Peter Young, took in the children.

Naismith excelled at physical activities and was an outstanding **athlete** in high school. He attended McGill University in Montreal and graduated in 1887. After graduation, he decided to become a minister and enrolled in a theological school. Naismith remained involved in athletics, though, and he especially enjoyed rough sports such as lacrosse and rugby. His teachers were dismayed by Naismith's interest in sports, but he believed that he could minister to young people through athletics.

Naismith explained his idea to the general secretary of the Young Men's Christian Association (YMCA) in Montreal. The secretary suggested he join the YMCA International Training School in Springfield, Massachusetts. Naismith took his advice and arrived at the school in 1891.

At that time, indoor physical education consisted mostly of repetitive exercises and drills. One of Naismith's teachers gave him an assignment, which was to create a game that could be played indoors.

At first, Naismith tried versions of soccer, rugby, and lacrosse, but they were too rough for indoor play. Then, Naismith developed a new game that would involve handling and passing a large ball and using it to score in a high, horizontal goal. He nailed two peach baskets suspended from the balconies at either end of the gym, divided his class of young men into two teams, gave them a soccer ball, and came up with the original thirteen rules of his new game.

Naismith's game, which soon earned the name **basketball**, was an immediate success. Some adjustments were made, such as using a different ball, cutting the bottoms out of the baskets so the ball would fall through, and allowing players to dribble the ball as they ran up the floor.

Naismith went on to earn several doctoral degrees. In 1894, he married Maud Sherman, and they had five children. The family later moved to Kansas, where Naismith became the director of Kansas University's physical education department. In 1915, Naismith became a Presbyterian minister, and in 1925, he became a U.S. citizen.

James Naismith died of a heart attack on November 28, 1939. In 1968, basketball honored its founder by establishing the **Naismith Memorial Basketball Hall of Fame**, in Springfield, Massachusetts.

◆ **HELENA RUBINSTEIN** believed in the beauty of a woman's face. Starting with a few jars of face cream and a dream, she created a **cosmetics** empire that became one of America's most famous corporations.

The oldest of eight children, Helena Rubinstein was born in Kraków, Poland, on December 25, 1870. When Helen and her sisters were young girls, their mother would apply cream to their faces, telling them it would help make them beautiful. After high school, Helena enrolled in medical school with the hope of becoming a doctor. However, while she loved the lab work, she dreaded the prospect of constantly being around sick people.

In 1902, Rubinstein emigrated to Australia to live with relatives. She noticed that many women in that country had rough, red faces from the hot sun and dry weather. Rubinstein soon introduced her friends and neighbors to a **face cream** developed by a chemist named Jacob Lyusky. The cream was so popular that Rubinstein decided to go into business, and with the help of a $1,500 loan, she opened a small **cosmetics shop** in the city of Melbourne. Rubinstein sat down with each woman and instructed her on the best ways to care for her skin. Customers loved this individual attention, and Rubinstein's shop soon became a huge success.

In 1908, Rubinstein opened another shop in London, England. While in London, she met Edward Titus, an American journalist working in Europe. The couple soon married and went on to have two sons. The family lived in Paris, France, where Rubinstein ran a popular beauty salon, but they fled to the United States when World War I broke out in 1914.

Rubinstein continued to expand her business in her new home. In order to continue the individual attention for which she was known, she personally trained salespeople to teach women skin care techniques.

Rubinstein's marriage to Titus had been unhappy for some time, and they divorced in 1937. The following year, she married a Russian prince named Artchil Gourielli-Tchkonia. She later developed a line of skin care products for men that she named after the prince. The two remained married until his death in 1955.

Rubinstein became incredibly wealthy, and while she did spend some of her fortune on priceless paintings and sculptures, she also put much of her wealth to good use. She donated large sums of money to support Israel and to encourage students to study Jewish culture and history. In 1953, she founded the **Helena Rubinstein Foundation** to support health care, medical research, and other charitable causes.

In 1959, Rubinstein represented the United States cosmetics industry at an international exhibition in the Soviet Union. She continued to run her foundation until her death in New York City on April 1, 1965.

The early years of the twentieth century saw the birth of a new industry—**automobile manufacturing**—that would revolutionize American transportation. One man who helped shape this new industry and lead one of the giant U.S. automakers to prominence during the 1920s and '30s was a Danish immigrant named **WILLIAM KNUDSEN**.

Signius Wilhelm Knudsen was born in Copenhagen, Denmark, on March 25, 1879. The young man had a knack for working with machines, and by his late teens, he had a job as a bicycle mechanic. However, Knudsen dreamed of a better life in America, and he emigrated to New York City in 1900.

He changed his name to the more American-sounding William S. Knudsen and worked at various shipyards and railroad yards before getting a job at the **Keim Mills** in Buffalo, New York, which made steel parts for the automotive industry. In 1911, Knudsen married, and he and his wife Clara went on to have three daughters and a son.

In 1913, the **Ford Motor Company**, which had bought Keim two years earlier, asked Knudsen to come to Detroit, Michigan, to expand the company's assembly plants. Knudsen quickly got a reputation as a tough boss who could yell, "Hurry up!" at workers in fifteen languages. During World War I, Knudsen directed Ford's production of submarine-chasing boats. By 1920, Knudsen was in charge of Ford's European business.

However, Knudsen often clashed with company owner **Henry Ford**, who was just as strong-willed as Knudsen. In 1921, Knudsen quit Ford and went to work as the manager of a Detroit auto parts factory. The following year, rival car company, **General Motors** (GM), offered him a job. Within a month, he was promoted to vice president of GM's **Chevrolet Motor Company**, and by 1924, he was president. Under Knudsen's leadership, Chevrolet became the number one car company in America during the 1930s, and by 1937, he was president of General Motors.

During the early 1940s, with the United States at war, the focus of American industrial production involved making equipment for the military. **President Franklin D. Roosevelt** asked Knudsen to join the government's Council of National Defense, and Knudsen accepted the unpaid position, giving up his annual salary of $300,000.

By 1943, Knudsen was the director of production for the War Department. Roosevelt also appointed him to the rank of lieutenant general in the army—the first time this honor was given to a civilian. Knudsen helped war production run smoothly, and in 1944, he was awarded the Army's Distinguished Service Medal.

In 1945, Knudsen wanted to return to his position at General Motors. However, he had reached the mandatory retirement age of sixty-five and was forced to resign. Brokenhearted, Knudsen left the company.

William Knudsen died on April 27, 1948, in Detroit, Michigan.

SAMUEL GOLDWYN was an immigrant twice over. When he finally reached America, though, his life took a turn that surprised everyone—including him.

The man who would become one of the most famous movie moguls in Hollywood was born Schmuel Gelbfisz in the Jewish ghetto of Warsaw, in Russian Poland, on August 27, 1879. His family was very poor and, like other Jews, suffered persecution at the hands of the Russian government.

After Schmuel's father died around 1893, the boy traveled to Birmingham, England, to live with relatives. He also anglicized his name to Samuel Goldfish and worked at various jobs to earn money to emigrate to America.

Goldfish arrived in New York when he was about sixteen years old and moved to Gloversville, New York. The town was well known for glove making, and for the next few years, Goldfish worked in a **glove factory**. In 1902, he became a U.S. citizen.

Goldfish worked for a while as a **traveling salesman** and later became the manager of another glove company. By 1912, he was making $15,000 a year, an enormous salary for that time, and living an elegant life. Unfortunately, he was bored.

Goldfish had become a fan of the theater and movies, and he and his brother-in-law, Jesse Lasky, and another partner named Cecil B. DeMille, started their own film company called the Feature Play Company. Goldfish's job was to find buyers for the movies that the company made. He was very successful, but his partners objected when he wanted to take a bigger role as a producer and administrator.

In 1916, Goldfish left to start another company with the Selwyn family, who were famous theater producers. They combined their names to create a new company name: Goldwyn. Goldfish liked the name so much that he legally changed his name to Samuel Goldwyn in 1918. In 1922, the Goldwyn studio merged with another film company to create what would become the most famous movie studio in Hollywood history: **Metro-Goldwyn-Mayer** (MGM).

In 1924, Goldwyn sold his interest in MGM and became an independent producer, a role he kept for thirty-five years. Goldwyn personally financed and supervised his films, making them at his own studio and distributing them through **United Artists Corporation** and **RKO Radio Pictures**.

During his career, Goldwyn was a colorful figure in Hollywood, known for his malapropisms and somewhat garbled but expressive language. He was responsible for some of Hollywood's most successful and acclaimed movies, including *Wuthering Heights* (1939), *The Little Foxes* (1941), and *The Best Years of Our Lives* (1946), which won seven Academy Awards, including Best Picture.

Goldwyn retired in 1959 and lived quietly with his second wife, Frances. In 1969, he suffered a stroke that confined him to a wheelchair. His health continued to fail, and he died on January 31, 1974.

Was **JOE HILL** a criminal or a martyr? The verdict is still out on this songwriter and symbol of the American **labor movement**.

He was born Joel Emmanuel Hägglund, in Gävle, Sweden, on October 7, 1879, the ninth child of a railroad worker. When his father died soon after his eighth birthday, he left school and got a job shoveling coal to help support his family.

When Hägglund was twenty-three years old, his mother died. He and his brother Paul left Sweden for America, arriving in New York City in October 1902. Even though he knew how to speak English, the only job Hägglund could find was cleaning bar spittoons for a few pennies a day.

Hägglund left New York and spent the next eight years wandering the western United States. He became involved in the growing labor movement, and it is rumored that he also committed petty crimes. Sometime between 1906 and 1910, Joel Hägglund decided to change his name to protect himself. He began using the name Joseph Hillstrom, which he later shortened to Joe Hill.

During this time, Hill joined a new union called the **Industrial Workers of the World** (IWW). The IWW advocated a radical approach within the labor movement. Its goal was to take profits away from the wealthy and place them directly into the hands of the workers.

Between 1909 and 1912, Hill traveled around the United States recruiting IWW members and taking part in many job actions. Hill was a self-taught musician who could play piano, guitar, and violin, and he used his songwriting talents to promote the cause.

Hill's labor efforts often got him in trouble with the law, and he spent time in jail. Then, in January 1914, when he was staying with friends in Salt Lake City, Utah, Hill was arrested for the double murder of two shopkeepers. At Hill's trial, the prosecution admitted it only had circumstantial evidence that merely implicated Hill, and that they could not provide a plausible motive linking him to the crime. Despite this, the jury found him guilty, and he was sentenced to death.

The IWW and other supporters of the workers' movement claimed Big Business had orchestrated Hill's charges and conviction. Thousands of petitions, telegrams, and letters were sent to Utah officials, including the governor, asking to commute the sentence to life in prison. The Swedish ambassador to the United States and AFL President Samuel Gompers (see no. 14) both made personal appeals to **President Woodrow Wilson**, claiming that Hill had not received a fair trial.

However, all appeals failed, and Hill was executed by firing squad on November 19, 1915. The night before his execution, Hill sent a message to IWW leaders, and it became a rallying cry for workers and protesters for generations: "Don't waste any time mourning. Organize!"

AMALIE EMMY NOETHER was a woman of unbreakable spirit and personal drive, whose love for the field of **mathematics** brought her acclaim as one of the most celebrated mathematicians of modern times.

Born on March 23, 1882, in Erlangen, Germany, Emmy Noether's passion for learning came to her early. Her father Max Noether, a professor and mathematician himself, spared no expense in young Emmy's education. As a student, Emmy primarily studied German, French, and English with the intention of becoming a language teacher. Despite passing her teacher's examinations with flying colors, however, Noether never taught language classes. Instead, she decided to follow a much different and immensely more difficult path—mathematics.

For young women in the early 1900s, this was a nearly impossible pursuit, as women were only allowed to study mathematics unofficially in Germany, and only with the direct permission of each individual professor. Undeterred, Emmy Noether audited every class she could between the years of 1900 and 1902, eagerly learning everything available within the lectures. In 1904, after the rules regarding women in education were changed, Noether became one of the first women to be fully admitted to Erlangen University, where she redoubled her studies into mathematics and quickly proved herself to be one of the brightest minds of her generation. By 1907, Emmy Noether had completed her doctorate in the field of mathematics.

After her schooling, Noether continued her work and research at Erlangen University, assisting her father in many of his own tasks and studies. Soon, though, word of her brilliant and creative approach to mathematics had spread, and by 1915, she had been invited to help explore and verify many of the formulas within **Albert Einstein's** legendary theory of **general relativity**. Over the next two decades, Noether continued to produce some of the finest mathematical research and papers of her age in addition to lecturing at many universities throughout Germany.

In 1933, however, with the rise of the Nazis in Germany, Noether and many other Jewish academics were immediately removed from their academic positions across the country. Unwilling to give up her life's passion, Emmy left for the United States to continue her work. There, she quickly found guest teaching positions at universities such as Princeton, who were eager to hire such a respected and brilliant mathematician. Unfortunately, only two years after coming to the United States, she passed away. Today, she is remembered within the mathematics community as one of the single most inventive and creative minds to have ever worked within the field. Her unwavering determination to pursue what she loved—no matter the odds—has inspired countless others to do the same.

◆ **BELA LUGOSI** was a Hungarian American actor who was best known for his legendary performances in **horror films** in the early twentieth century. Forced to flee his country due to war and political danger, Bela made a new life in America and became one of its most beloved actors.

Born Blasko Béla Ferenc Dezső on October 20, 1882, in what is now Hungary near the western border of Transylvania, Bela had a fascination for the theater and acting even as a very young child. He often avoided schoolwork to practice his stage skills. When Bela's father disagreed with this behavior, Bela Lugosi decided to leave home and begin his acting career.

By the time he was only eighteen years old, Lugosi had already begun acting in theater productions across Hungary. In 1913, his reputation as a talented and dedicated actor had grown so much that he was invited to join the National Theatre, a very prestigious organization. Later, he showed his strong character when World War I began. Even though actors were not required to serve in the military, Lugosi willingly joined in order to help protect his country, and he was wounded while deployed in Russia. After World War I ended, the political situation in Hungary grew perilous.

By 1919, Bela Lugosi's life was in danger, and he was forced to leave his home. While Lugosi lived for some time in both Vienna, Austria, and in Germany, he eventually worked as a sailor so that he could emigrate to the United States. In America, Lugosi quickly returned to his passion of acting, and audiences grew to love him. In the 1920s, he began to work in both stage plays and silent films.

Of all his roles, though, none were as popular as when he played Count Dracula on Broadway in a stage adaptation of Bram Stoker's novel, *Dracula*. For thirty-three weeks, Bela Lugosi took to the stage and *became* the legendary vampire. The play was an enormous success, and soon Lugosi began working on Hollywood movies. Throughout the years, he played many different roles in many different types of movies, but he was always remembered most strongly as a perfect Count Dracula. Even today, when horror film fans think of the legendary vampire, they think of Bela Lugosi first.

Lugosi lived an amazing life and overcame many challenges and tragedies in order to chase his lifelong dreams. When he first came to the United States, he owned almost nothing, but with his unbreakable spirit and amazing determination, he built himself the life he had always dreamed of.

FELIX FRANKFURTER came to the United States as a young boy who did not speak a word of English. He grew up to become a distinguished Harvard University law professor and went on to shape the laws of his adopted country as an associate justice on the **U.S. Supreme Court**.

Felix Frankfurter was born into an Orthodox Jewish family in Vienna, Austria, on November 15, 1882. In 1894, his family immigrated to the United States and settled in New York. Frankfurter did not know any English, but he learned the language as quickly as possible, and soon became a top student at school.

After graduating from the City College of New York with high honors in 1902, Frankfurter worked for New York City's Housing Department for a year. Then, he enrolled in Harvard Law School, where he graduated first in his class in 1906. He worked as a **lawyer** in private practice for a short time, but his intense interest in politics soon led him in a new direction.

Frankfurter spent three years as assistant to **U.S. Attorney Henry Stimson** for New York. When **President William Howard Taft** appointed Stimson as secretary of war, Frankfurter followed him to Washington, DC, and got a job as legal counsel in the **War Department**.

In 1914, Frankfurter joined the faculty of Harvard Law School, where he remained until 1939. In 1919, he married Marion Denman, the daughter of a Presbyterian minister. The couple had no children.

During the 1920s, Frankfurter became known for his progressive views and his willingness to criticize injustices wherever he saw them. He was very outspoken in the controversial Nicola Sacco and Bartolomeo Vanzetti case, lending his support to the unsuccessful appeal for the Italian immigrants, who many people believed had been unfairly convicted of murder and who were subsequently executed.

After **President Franklin D. Roosevelt** took office in 1932, Frankfurter's life took a new turn. Although he remained on the faculty of Harvard, Frankfurter became one of Roosevelt's most trusted advisers.

In 1939, Roosevelt appointed Frankfurter to be an **associate justice** on the Supreme Court. He became only the third Jewish justice, and the first naturalized citizen to serve on the Court.

During his twenty-three years on the Court, Frankfurter was a firm believer in judicial restraint, and his votes sometimes puzzled and disappointed his longtime progressive allies. His decisions often deferred to the actions of the executive and legislative branches of government, but other times, he sided with the rights of minorities who claimed they were being harmed by unjust laws.

Frankfurter resigned from the Supreme Court in 1962, after suffering a stroke. He died three years later, on February 22, 1965.

KHALIL GIBRAN was a Lebanese American **author and poet** who created some of the most beautiful writing of the early twentieth century. Even long after his life was over, many of his works remained hugely popular.

Born on January 6, 1883, in Bsharrī, Lebanon, Gibran demonstrated an emotional intelligence and passion for art even as a very young boy. Although he grew up in an area where schooling was rare and inconsistent, Gibran was sharp and hungry to learn.

In 1895, when Khalil was only twelve years old, he and his family immigrated to their new home in Boston, Massachusetts. There, Gibran enrolled for the first time in a real school. Although he was a very good student in general, he especially loved his art classes. Because of his natural talent, he was sent to be mentored by Fred Holland Day, a well-known photographer.

Gibran moved backed to Lebanon when he was a teenager to attend a different school. There, he began studying poetry and helped create a student magazine at school. In 1901 and 1902, however, Gibran suffered great tragedy when his sister, brother, and mother all passed away. He returned to the United States and refocused his efforts on art.

For some time, Gibran wrote weekly poetry for an Arabic newspaper column, and he drew small pictures to match each poem. In 1905, he expanded his work and published many of his short stories. But by 1911, Gibran had moved to New York City where his artistic career truly began to take off. He was surrounded by other artists and their art, and he was inspired. He continued to create his own art of many different types, from beautiful **paintings** to **poetry** and **novels**.

In 1923, after publishing many novels to moderate success, Khalil Gibran wrote and published his book *The Prophet*. The novel was Gibran's first big success as an author, and it sold out very quickly. With *The Prophet*, Gibran's reputation as a talented writer grew enormously, and soon he was invited to join the **New Orient Society**. An organization for famous authors, the group helped give Gibran a place where he was around people like himself. Over the next decade, Khalil Gibran continued to write many best-selling books, which are still read and loved today. Today, he is recognized as the third best-selling poet in history.

As a boy in Austria, **ROBERT HARRY LOWIE** loved to read tales of cowboys and Indians in the American West. As an adult, he became one of the world's greatest scholars of **American Indians**.

Robert Harry Lowie was born on June 12, 1883, in Vienna. Growing up, Lowie loved to read, and his favorite books were about America. He enjoyed James Fenimore Cooper's *Leatherstocking Tales*, as well as cheap paperback books about the Comanche and Apache tribes. He also was obsessed with the idea of traveling, and he spent hours poring over maps and dreaming of faraway places.

When he was ten years old, Lowie's travel dreams came true when his family immigrated to New York City. Lowie continued his education in the New York City schools and went on to graduate from City College when he was only eighteen years old.

Lowie was proficient at languages, but he had no idea what to do with his life until he read about a new anthropology department at New York's Columbia University. To pay for his education, he taught fourth grade while he worked toward degrees in anthropology and psychology. He also volunteered at the **American Museum of Natural History** and wrote magazine articles.

In 1906, one of Lowie's professors invited him to study the **Lemhi Shoshone tribe** in central Idaho. Lowie jumped at the chance and made the difficult journey west. However, he found that nothing in his life up till then had prepared him for life among the Indians.

One of his biggest challenges was learning to ride a horse so that he could travel among his subjects' distant homes. Learning the Shoshone language was also very difficult, especially since there was no written form to study.

After he finished his assignment with the Shoshone, Lowie went on to study the **Blackfeet Nation, Assiniboine, and Crow tribes**. He especially treasured his time with the Crow, and for the rest of his career, he returned to their communities again and again, becoming extremely fluent in their language.

Lowie studied other tribes as well, and spent more time living among the American Indians than any other anthropologist. In addition to his fieldwork, Lowie served as a professor at the University of California, Berkeley, from 1921 to 1950, where he started a graduate program in anthropology. Lowie wrote more than three hundred articles about his work with the tribes and penned many books, including *Culture and Ethnology* and *Introduction to Cultural Anthropology*.

Robert Harry Lowie died on September 21, 1957, having fulfilled his childhood dream of studying and living among the American Indian tribes.

◆ **ELIZABETH ARDEN** was born a poor farm girl in rural Canada. She went on to change her home, her name, and her fortune to become one of the most successful **women in business** in America.

Elizabeth Arden was born on December 31, 1884, in the tiny village of Woodbridge, Canada. Her birth name was Florence Nightingale Graham, after the famous nurse. The Grahams owned a small farm, and the family—Florence had four siblings—was happy but did not have much money. Things took a turn for the worse, however, when Florence was six years old because her mother died of tuberculosis.

Florence's father managed to care for his children despite the loss of his wife. In her mid-teens, Florence moved to the city of Toronto to study nursing, but she discovered she hated nursing school. Instead, she dreamed of creating her own **skin creams** as beauty aids for women.

Florence lived in Toronto until she was thirty years old and worked at a variety of office jobs. Dissatisfied with her life, she decided to move to New York City and get a job in the beauty industry. She worked in several salons, applying face creams and learning everything she could about the business.

By 1910, she was ready to start her own business. She was also ready to change her name to something shorter and more glamorous. Florence Nightingale Graham became Elizabeth Arden.

Arden opened a **beauty salon** in one of New York City's most fashionable neighborhoods and soon acquired a well-to-do clientele. Arden made sure these women were pampered at her salon, and she created a luxurious and relaxing environment—a place that women would look forward to visiting. The business was immediately successful thanks to Arden's hard work— she routinely put in twelve-hour days—and her knack for marketing her products and creating a stylish image.

In 1914, Arden went to the bank to get a loan to expand her company. She got the loan and fell in love with the banker, Thomas Lewis. They married in 1917. Lewis used his financial expertise to expand Arden's business around the world.

Arden's company was the driving force in her life. Her marriage became more of a business partnership, and the couple did not have any children. Arden was known as a demanding woman, and she eventually divorced her husband and cut ties with several family members.

Arden continued to run her business until her death on October 19, 1966. Her desire to control everything meant that no one was left to run the business after she died. As a result, the firm was bought by the drug company Eli Lilly, which continued to sell cosmetics and promote glamour under the famous **Elizabeth Arden** name.

LUDWIG MIES VAN DER ROHE believed that "less is more." He used this principle to become one of the most innovative and important **architects** of the twentieth century.

Ludwig Mies was born on March 27, 1886, in Aachen, Germany. His father was a master stonemason, and Mies worked with him from childhood. Mies also apprenticed with a local draftsman to learn the basics of architectural design.

When he was nineteen years old, Mies moved to Berlin, Germany, and began working for a leading German furniture designer. Although he soon moved on to designing buildings, Mies realized he needed more training. In 1908, he became an apprentice to Peter Behrens, one of the most creative architects and designers in Germany. Mies was heavily influenced by Behrens's use of modern technology to create stunning, innovative buildings.

Mies married in 1913, but the marriage ended in 1921. He then changed his name to Mies van der Rohe (van der Rohe was his mother's maiden name). After World War I ended in 1918, Mies began studying skyscrapers and became fascinated with their tall, sleek design. During the next ten years, he had five major architectural exhibits in Germany, and in 1929, van der Rohe designed one of his most famous buildings, the **German Pavilion** for the International Exhibition in Barcelona, Spain. The one-story structure was simple and sophisticated.

After Adolf Hitler came to power in Germany during the 1930s, van der Rohe decided to leave the country. He settled in Chicago, Illinois, where he was appointed director of the city's Armour Institute (present-day Illinois Institute of Technology). For the next twenty years, van der Rohe was responsible not only for all the academic programs at the school, but also for planning the campus and designing many of its buildings. The campus reflects van der Rohe's preference for steel-framed buildings with glass or yellow brick panels.

Later in his career, van der Rohe turned to furniture design, for which he is best known. One of his most famous creations was the **Barcelona chair and stool**, featuring an x-shaped, supporting steel frame with leather cushions. Experts still consider this chair one of the most beautifully designed pieces of the twentieth century.

Along with his work for the Armour Institute, van der Rohe designed many other notable buildings, including the **Lake Shore Drive Apartments** in Chicago, the **Seagram Building** in New York City, and the **Farnsworth House** in Plano, Illinois. Van der Rohe, who became a U.S. citizen in 1944, received numerous honors and awards during his lifetime, including the Presidential Medal of Freedom in 1963.

Van der Rohe died in Chicago on August 17, 1969. He is still honored today as one of the leading pioneers of modern architecture.

America's youth found a true friend in **FATHER EDWARD FLANAGAN**. This Irish priest took in thousands of unwanted or troubled boys and began a **child welfare institution** that has been in existence for more than eighty-five years.

Edward Joseph Flanagan was born on a farm near Ballymoe, Ireland, on July 13, 1886. As was common for the time, his family had many children and little money. They relied on their staunch Catholic faith to get them through hard times.

In 1904, eighteen-year-old Flanagan and his brother sailed to America to begin a new life in New York City. Flanagan wanted to become a priest, and he enrolled in St. Joseph's Seminary in New York. After studying abroad in Italy and Austria, he was ordained in 1912.

For the next five years, Flanagan served at several parishes in and around Omaha, Nebraska. He became interested in the plight of people experiencing homelessness and delinquent children, many of whom were abandoned or neglected by their parents. "The poor, innocent, unfortunate little children belong to us, and it is our problem to give them every chance to develop into good men and good women," he once said.

In 1917, the Omaha courts awarded custody of five young homeless boys to Flanagan. He borrowed ninety dollars and rented a home in the city, which he named Father Flanagan's Boys' Home. Six months later, he moved his boys into a larger house, and in 1921, he purchased a farm near Omaha so he could take in more children.

To support his boys, Father Flanagan printed a newsletter and spoke on the radio. In 1926, the name of the organization was officially changed to **Boys Town**. By 1938, Boys Town was so well known that a movie about Father Flanagan and his boys became a huge box-office success.

Father Flanagan fervently believed that, "There are no bad boys." He blamed delinquent behavior on bad parenting and a bad environment and said, "There is nothing the matter with our growing boys that love, proper training, and guidance will not remedy." Flanagan also did not hesitate to take in boys of all races and religions at a time when segregation and prejudice were accepted in society.

In 1947, the War Department invited Father Flanagan to tour Japan and Korea and advise the United States on how war orphans could be helped. Later, Flanagan traveled to Germany to assist war orphans there as well. While in Berlin, he suffered a heart attack and died on May 15, 1948. His body was sent back to Boys Town for burial.

Today, Boys Town continues to follow Father Flanagan's mission to help disadvantaged youths and provide a brighter future for "all God's children."

During the 1920s, America discovered a new **college football** powerhouse, the "Fighting Irish" of **Notre Dame University**. The man who brought the school to football dominance was a Norwegian immigrant who became a coaching legend— **KNUTE ROCKNE**.

Knute Rockne was born on March 4, 1888, in the small community of Voss, Norway. In 1889, Rockne's father, a carriage-maker, immigrated to Chicago, Illinois. Soon afterward, he sent for his wife, his son Knute, and Knute's three sisters to join him.

Rockne spent much of his time playing sports in the streets and empty lots of the city. His favorite sport was football, which he played both in the neighborhood and on his high school team. After high school, Rockne worked as a mail dispatcher in the Chicago Post Office and continued playing football at local athletic clubs. After four years, he saved enough money to enroll at Notre Dame in South Bend, Illinois, choosing the school because two of his friends were also going there.

Rockne became a member of the school's All-America football squad and served as team captain during his senior year. Rockne also studied hard, edited the school yearbook, played the flute, and ran for the school's track team—all while working as a janitor and a chemistry research assistant to pay his way through school.

After he graduated in 1914, Notre Dame offered Rockne a job as a graduate assistant in chemistry. He accepted the position on the condition that he could also be assistant coach of the football team. In 1917, Rockne became the team's **head coach**.

Under Rockne's direction, Notre Dame became one of college football's dominant teams. Over the next thirteen years, Notre Dame had five unbeaten and untied seasons, and won the **1925 Rose Bowl**. Rockne also coached twenty-first team All-Americans and achieved a lifetime winning percentage of .881, still one of the best records in college football.

Rockne was the first coach to take his players all over the country, challenging the best teams he could find. In doing so, the "Fighting Irish" gained fans throughout the nation. Rockne was famous for his tough, take-no-prisoners attitude and his fiery half-time speeches to inspire his team. Rockne also designed his own equipment and uniforms, emphasized the passing game, and introduced a play called the "shift" where all four running backs were in motion when the ball was snapped to the receiver.

By the early 1930s, Rockne was a nationally known and widely admired figure. But America was stunned when, on March 31, 1931, the hero was killed in a plane crash.

In 1940, a Hollywood film was made about Rockne's life. He remains one of the greatest coaches and figures in college football history.

Few composers have had as much influence on American music as **IRVING BERLIN**. From Broadway musicals to movies to popular songs, this Russian immigrant wrote more hit songs in a greater variety of musical styles than any other American **composer**.

Berlin was born Israel Baline on May 11, 1888, in Mogilyov, Russia (present-day Belarus), the youngest of six children of a Jewish cantor and his wife. When Israel was five years old, the family moved to the Lower East Side of New York City. Berlin's father died when the boy was thirteen, and he turned to various jobs to help support his family. He worked as a singing waiter in a Chinatown café and a street performer who sang for pennies. However, his future lay in songwriting. He published his first song, "Marie from Sunny Italy," in 1907, and a printer's error on the sheet music gave him the name Irving Berlin, which he decided to keep professionally.

In 1911, Berlin published "Alexander's Ragtime Band," for which he wrote both the words and music, and it went on to become a huge hit. After that, Berlin wrote more than fifteen hundred songs, including such classics as "Puttin' on the Ritz," "White Christmas," and "There's No Business Like Show Business." Perhaps his best-known song is the classic tribute to his adopted country, "**God Bless America**."

Berlin also wrote the music for many **Broadway shows**, including *Annie Get Your Gun*, and classic movies such as *Top Hat*, *Holiday Inn*, and *Easter Parade*. A sharp entrepreneur, Berlin cofounded ASCAP, or the **American Society of Composers, Authors, and Publishers**, which became one of the two main organizations for songwriting royalties.

Despite his prolific songwriting, Berlin was only of modest talent as a musician. He was a self-taught pianist with very limited skills and had only the most fundamental understanding of music composition.

In 1912, Berlin married Dorothy Goetz, but she died just five months later. In 1926, he was the center of a scandal when he eloped with Ellin Mackay, an author and the daughter of a telegraph company executive who opposed the marriage. Berlin and Mackay had three daughters as well as a son who died shortly after birth, and they remained devoted to each other until her death in 1988.

During his career, Berlin showed his appreciation to the country in which he enjoyed such great success. He donated all the profits from "God Bless America" to the Boy Scouts and Girl Scouts, and he gave all the proceeds from his song "This Is the Army" to the U.S. government.

In 1977, Berlin was awarded the Presidential Medal of Freedom in recognition of his many contributions to American culture. Irving Berlin died on September 22, 1989, at the age of 101.

◆ **CHARLIE CHAPLIN** emerged from a sad, deprived childhood in England to create one of the most beloved characters in Hollywood film history.

Charles Spencer Chaplin was born in London on April 16, 1889, to a music hall singer and an actress. Chaplin's parents divorced when he was very young, and his mother supported Charles and his older half brother Sidney by taking up sewing. When Charles was seven years old, his mother was committed to a psychiatric hospital, and he and Sidney were sent to a workhouse.

Chaplin first toured with a stage company when he was nine years old, and he continued acting and singing throughout his teens. In 1910, Chaplin and his brother toured the United States as part of a **vaudeville** team called the Karno Troupe. Two years later, the Karno Troupe returned, and Chaplin decided to remain in America.

Chaplin's movie career began in 1913 when he joined Mack Sennett's Keystone Film Studio, a studio best known for slapstick comedies. Chaplin appeared in his first film, *Making a Living,* in 1914. He also introduced his unique character, The Little Tramp. The antics of this sad but resilient fellow with a small mustache and funny gait made him an audience favorite, and Chaplin was soon famous all over the world.

In 1915, Chaplin left Keystone and joined another studio, Essanay. However, Chaplin wanted more control over his work, and to achieve this, in 1919, he became cofounder with actors Douglas Fairbanks and Mary Pickford along with director D. W. Griffith of United Artists.

In 1921, Chaplin released his first full-length movie, *The Kid.* It became an instant classic. For the next fifteen years, Chaplin wrote, directed, and starred in several brilliant silent movies, including *The Gold Rush* (1925), *City Lights* (1931) and *Modern Times* (1936).

Despite the advent of sound pictures in 1927, Chaplin continued to make silent movies into the late 1930s. He began using spoken dialogue in 1940 with **The Great Dictator**, a satire on Adolf Hitler and fascism. His last American film was *Limelight* (1952).

Chaplin's off-screen activities often made headlines. He married and divorced several women much younger than he was, and his popularity suffered as a result. Accusations of paternity suits—often unproven—and his left-leaning political views ultimately cost him his residence in the United States.

In 1951, while Chaplin was on his way to England, the U.S. Department of State notified him that it had rescinded his reentry permit. Chaplin then settled in Switzerland, where he lived for the rest of his life. In 1972, he returned to the United States to receive a special Academy Award.

Chaplin's last marriage was to his fourth wife, Oona O'Neil, the young daughter of playwright Eugene O'Neil. It lasted thirty-four years until Chaplin's death on December 25, 1977.

In the 1930s, popular magazine ads showed a "97-pound weakling" getting sand kicked in his face on the beach before transforming into a perfect physical powerhouse. These ads were based on a real incident that happened to bodybuilder **CHARLES ATLAS**, a man who built a career on promoting the benefits of becoming physically fit.

Charles Atlas was born Angelo Siciliano in Calabria, Italy, on October 30, 1892. When he was ten years old, he and his parents immigrated to the United States and settled in Brooklyn, New York. Young Angelo was not very interested in school, and in 1908, he left to work in a leather factory.

Frail and sickly, the young man was often beaten and humiliated by bullies. Angelo decided to improve his body but was disappointed when exercises failed to build up his muscles. Then, one day, he was watching a lion stretch and move at New York's Prospect Park Zoo. He realized that the animal's powerful muscles had been developed in a more natural way than lifting weights.

From this observation, Angelo developed a series of **isotonic exercises** that pitted one muscle against another to make the muscles stronger. These exercises transformed Angelo's body so much that friends began comparing him to a statue of Atlas, the figure from Greek mythology who holds up the world. In 1922, Angelo Siciliano legally changed his name to Charles Atlas.

Atlas began performing feats of strength in **vaudeville shows** and **circuses**. He also became a model and posed for about forty-five statues. After winning several **bodybuilding competitions**, Atlas used the prize money to open a mail-order business to market his exercise methods. However, Atlas was a poor businessperson, and the enterprise did not do well until he joined forces with Charles P. Roman, a young advertising executive.

Under Roman's management, the Atlas company prospered. Roman came up with the name "Dynamic-Tension" to describe Atlas's methods, and also created the advertising campaign featuring the "97-pound weakling." Atlas also promoted the company through public appearances and stunts, such as pulling railroad cars.

Along with promoting physical fitness, Atlas embodied the ideal of the self-made man. He promised not only to help young men change their bodies but also to increase their self-confidence and success. This program was eagerly adopted by millions of young men during the 1930s and 1940s.

Despite great financial success and international celebrity, Atlas lived a private, simple life consisting of exercise, work, and time with his family. In 1918, he married Margaret Cassano, and the couple had two children.

Atlas died of a heart attack on December 23, 1972. His company still exists today, dedicated to improving the lives through physical fitness.

He was "The Sheik" and "The Great Lover." Over a short career in **silent films, RUDOLPH VALENTINO** achieved a level of stardom that was unprecedented in his era.

Rudolph Valentino was born on May 6, 1895, in Castellaneta, Italy. Although his family lived comfortably, young Rudolph was bored with Italy and small town life. After getting into trouble at school, his mother finally gave in to Rudolph's begging and gave him the money his father had put way for his education. At the age of eighteen, Valentino set sail for the United States, arriving in New York on December 23, 1913.

At first, Valentino struggled in America, taking menial jobs while he learned English. A job as a gardener on a millionaire's estate gave Valentino the chance to study the manners and tastes of the rich, and he dreamed of achieving the same lifestyle for himself. Unfortunately, he neglected his work and was soon fired.

Valentino's luck changed when he found a job as a busboy at an Italian restaurant and cabaret. An older waiter befriended him and taught him to dance. Valentino became a dancer at the restaurant, and later he became the star attraction at Maxim's, a high-class dance club in New York.

After Valentino became involved in a scandalous relationship with a married woman, he decided to leave New York for Hollywood. Valentino's good looks and abundant charm soon caught the eye of a popular actress named Mae Murray, who cast him as the lead in several of her movies. His image as a mysterious loner attracted even more interest, and Valentino's career took off.

He won a coveted role in *The Four Horsemen of the Apocalypse* in 1921. Later that year, he starred in his career-defining role, in **The Sheik**, which cemented his status as "The Great Lover."

Valentino now had the extravagant lifestyle of which he had always dreamed. He was rich and popular, and appeared at Hollywood parties with a series of beautiful women on his arm. However, Valentino's personal life soon became unhappy and tumultuous. His marriage to Jean Acker soon ended in divorce. Valentino then married a Russian production designer named Natacha Rambova, but that marriage soon failed as well. Valentino's career continued to thrive, as he starred in *Blood and Sand* (1922), *The Eagle* (1925) and *Son of the Sheik* (1926). However, it all ended abruptly on August 15, 1926, when he was rushed to the hospital with acute appendicitis. An infection set in, and Rudolph Valentino died on August 23, 1926. He was only thirty-one years old.

Movie fans around the world mourned the loss of this Hollywood star, whose name today is still a symbol of the dashing icon of the silver screen.

GERTY RADNITZ CORI overcame many obstacles to succeed in a field dominated by men, and she went on to become the first American woman to receive a **Nobel Prize** in science.

Gerty Theresa Radnitz was born to a wealthy Jewish family in Prague, Czechoslovakia (present-day Czech Republic), on August 15, 1896. Gerty had private tutors until she was ten years old, and then she attended a finishing school.

Her uncle suggested Gerty attend medical school, but she faced a big problem. Girls had to pass tests in Latin, mathematics, and science in order to be admitted to the university, and no girls' school taught these subjects. Gerty spent a year studying on her own, though, and passed the admissions test in 1914.

Gerty fell in love with **biochemistry**, an exciting new field that applied the principles of chemistry to biological problems. She also fell in love with a fellow student named Carl Cori, and the two married in 1920.

Although Gerty had converted to Catholicism to marry Cori, both were concerned about the rampant anti-Semitism in Europe. In 1922, Carl received an offer of a job running a cancer laboratory in Buffalo, New York, and they moved to the United States. Gerty worked there as a **pathologist**, and the couple spent much of their time doing research and publishing articles.

The Coris studied how the body sends energy from one place to another. By 1929, they were able to describe how muscles and the liver work to convert glycogen to sugar and recycle the waste material lactic acid back into glycogen. This theory became known as the **Cori cycle** and had a great effect on the treatment of **diabetes**.

After nine years, the Coris decided to leave Buffalo. Although Carl received many offers from prestigious universities, he turned them down because all the schools refused to hire Gerty as well. Finally, in 1931, the couple accepted positions at the Washington University School of Medicine in St. Louis, Missouri.

Gerty was a tireless worker with a sharp tongue and no patience for wasting time. Although many researchers did not get along with her personally, they realized she was a brilliant scientist. By 1947, scientists from all over the world were coming to work in the Coris' lab.

The Nobel Prize Committee recognized Gerty's brilliance, too. In 1947, she and Carl were awarded the Nobel Prize for discovering the enzymes that convert glycogen into sugar and back again.

Although the Coris were thrilled at the honor, they were also dealing with a personal tragedy. Gerty had been diagnosed with an unusual and fatal type of anemia, and she would be dependent on blood transfusions for the rest of her life.

Gerty Radnitz Cori died on October 26, 1957.

Among all the powerful and inspiring **civil rights activists** in the early and mid-twentieth century, very few were as capable of getting the hard work done as **ROSE PESOTTA**. A tough-as-nails woman who refused to compromise her beliefs, she is one of the most iconic figures in modern American history.

Born on November 20, 1896, in what is now Ukraine to a family of Jewish merchants, Rose was a strong-willed person from very early on. After only two years of formal education, Rose dropped out of primary school when she was a young girl to help with the family business and work at home. Despite this, her parents invested in tutors to ensure that Rose was educated.

Rose became involved with leftist, anti-government groups that fought against Russia's growing tyranny. For much of her teenage and early adult years, Rose was very active in these politically rebellious groups.

When her parents informed Rose of their plans to arrange her marriage, however, Rose refused. Instead, in 1913, she left home and immigrated to the United States, where she settled in New York. Always a hard worker, Rose quickly found a job at local shirtwaist factories. There, she taught herself English with the help of friends and coworkers. Still an avid political activist, Rose soon began participating in local **unions**. Though she was young, Rose's strong personality and determination marked her as a leader, and by 1920, she had been elected to the Local 25 Union's executive board.

With her growing responsibilities came a need for higher education. After being elected, Rose attended numerous schools in order to better her understanding of politics and leadership. Rose's reputation in the 1920s continued to grow as she encountered more and more people. Interestingly, Rose possessed a unique ability to relate to almost anyone. Because of this, she earned the support of people from all different backgrounds. In 1933, during the **Dressmakers General Strike** in California, Rose called on Mexican workers using Spanish-language radio programs. This creativity increased her reputation even further.

Though Rose resigned from her union position in 1942, partly due to discrimination, Rose remained a prominent figure within union activities across the United States. By the time of her death in 1965, Rose Pesotta had distinguished herself as one of the toughest champions of the union America had ever seen. Her legacy as a woman who would never stop fighting for her beliefs inspired countless others both during and after her lifetime.

FRANK CAPRA came to the United States as a young boy at the turn of the twentieth century, and he went on to create some of Hollywood's most popular and enduring **movies** during America's bleakest days.

The youngest child in a large family, Frank Capra was born in Palermo, Italy, on May 19, 1897. The Capras immigrated to the United States in 1903 and settled in Los Angeles. After finishing high school, Capra worked his way through college, and graduated in 1918 with a degree in chemical engineering.

Capra joined the army during World War I, where he taught math to artillery officers. In 1922, Capra was looking for a job when he answered a classified ad for a director to film an actor reading poetry. He later moved to Hollywood to work for directors Mack Sennett and Hal Roach.

Capra's first big film success was *The Strong Man* (1926). In 1928, he directed *The Submarine,* the first sound picture produced by Columbia Studios. Unlike other directors, Capra said that he was not afraid of sound pictures because he "knew all about sound waves from freshman physics."

Capra's career soared during the 1930s. His successes from that decade include such classics as *It Happened One Night, Mr. Deeds Goes to Town, You Can't Take It With You, Meet John Doe,* and *Mr. Smith Goes to Washington.*

Capra's movies usually emphasized the goodness of the common man and featured ordinary, honest people battling against powerful but corrupt businessmen or politicians. With the United States experiencing **The Great Depression**, American audiences found Capra's optimism for good to triumph over evil a welcome tonic.

Capra worked with the era's best-known actors, including Clark Gable, Gary Cooper, Jimmy Stewart, Claudette Colbert, and Jean Arthur. Capra won three **Academy Awards** for Best Director for *It Happened One Night, Mr. Deeds Goes to Town,* and *You Can't Take It with You.*

During World War II, Capra served his adopted country by producing a series of documentary films for the War Department called *Why We Fight.*

In 1946, Capra made ***It's a Wonderful Life,*** which was not very successful at the time of its release. However, this film, about an angel who shows a despondent man the true value of his life, went on to become a Christmas classic and one of Capra's most beloved works.

By the 1950s, Capra's most successful days were behind him. His final two Hollywood films were *A Hole in the Head* (1959) and *Pocketful of Miracles* (1961).

In 1982, the American Film Institute honored Capra with its Life Achievement Award. Capra suffered a stroke in 1985 and remained in poor health until his death on September 3, 1991.

One of the twentieth century's most influential composers and the driving force behind much of the modern orchestra scene that we enjoy today, **GEORGE SZELL** was a man of unique talent whose dedication to his craft marked him as one of history's greatest **musicians**.

Born in Budapest, Hungary, on June 7, 1897, George Szell's natural musical talent was apparent from early on. After time spent training with renowned pianist Richard Robert, Szell toured Europe to display and strengthen his talent. At just eleven, he played his first performance in London, and so impressive was the young boy's skill that many newspapers confidently named him "the next Mozart."

Following his early introduction to the world of professional music, Szell's skill and reputation as a pianist, composer, and conductor continued to grow. In 1915, when Szell was only eighteen years old, he received a coveted appointment to the Berlin Royal Court Opera, where he made lifelong friends with respected composer Richard Strauss. In the years before World War II broke out across Europe, Szell toured with countless orchestras across the continent, to Russia, and to the United States. When war officially began, however, Szell made the decision to immigrate to the United States.

In the States, it was not long before Szell found work as a **conductor** at the famed Metropolitan Opera in New York City. He worked there for four years before he officially became a naturalized U.S. citizen. Following his new citizenship status, Szell changed professional venues, becoming the musical director of the Cleveland Orchestra. Small and underfunded but well respected, the Cleveland Orchestra quickly found new life under the guidance of Szell. Throughout the nearly thirty years in which George Szell led it, the Cleveland Orchestra grew from a talented but small organization to one of the leading orchestras in the country, rivaling even the largest halls in Boston and New York. More than anything, it was Szell's unrelenting dedication to quality and excellence that drove the Cleveland Orchestra to new heights, and many today believe that Szell's work in Cleveland helped propel American orchestral music to where it is today.

Today, George Szell's legacy as a musical titan across Europe and the United States is almost unrivaled in the twentieth century, and he is remembered as a man who managed to produce unimaginable beauty during some of history's darkest years.

Among **human rights activists and suffragists**, few names carry as much weight and influence as that of **MABEL PING-HUA LEE**, whose tireless campaigning and activism in the early 1900s immensely helped ensure equal rights for all in the United States.

Born on October 7, 1897, in Canton City (present-day Guangzhou), China, Mabel Ping-Hua Lee spent her early childhood with her mother and grandmother in China, where she excelled in school. So impressive were her achievements that the young Mabel was awarded the prestigious Boxer Indemnity Scholarship, which gave her family the opportunity to immigrate to the United States. There, the Lee family found a new home in New York City, where Mabel attended Erasmus Hall Academy and continued to excel.

Her academic pursuits, however, were not the extent of her excellence. From an extraordinarily young age, Mabel found a calling and talent for activism. Not content with using her education and opportunity for her own gain, Mabel Ping-Hua Lee quickly began participating in the growing women's rights movement within New York, and by the age of only sixteen, she began helping lead parades for the cause. Becoming the topic of articles in *New York Tribune* and *New York Times*, the young Chinese immigrant soon rose to be one of the most recognizable faces of the suffragette movement.

Despite her fierce activism for women's rights, Mabel Ping-Hua Lee and other women of color were especially vulnerable to discrimination. Even after the movement succeeded in forcing the **Nineteenth Amendment**, which ensured equal voting rights for women, Mabel and others like her were still denied many such rights based on the color of their skin.

Still, Mabel persevered, continuing her education and using her impressive talents for writing and speaking by authoring countless feminist essays for collegiate magazines. Her continued work in the pursuit of social justice earned her recognition by the Women's Political Suffrage Shop, which invited her to speak to their organization when she was only nineteen years old.

An amazing force for change and justice in the early twentieth century, Mabel Ping-Hua Lee faced incredible odds and nearly overwhelming personal hardship during her lifetime, fighting for the rights of others even while she was denied those rights for herself. One of America's most cherished and respected civil rights activists, Lee helped to ensure a better future for her own generation and beyond, and her story continues to inspire countless others who believe in justice for all.

◆ **ETTORE BOIARDI**, perhaps better known as **"Chef Boyardee,"** was a chef and business-person who came to America as a young man and rose to become a household name.

Born on October 22, 1897, in Piacenza, Italy, Ettore began working in kitchens and restaurants when he was still a young child. Although, at first, he was only an assistant who fetched ingredients and washed dishes, he was a very hard worker who slowly worked his way to better positions. When Ettore was only eleven years old, he earned the position of apprentice chef at an Italian restaurant named La Croce Bianca. There, Ettore learned many of the skills which would help him be successful later in life.

When he was still a teenager, Ettore worked in restaurants in both London, England, and Paris, France, where he con-tinued to improve his skills and experience. At the age of sixteen, Ettore immigrated to the United States to begin working in a restaurant with his brother. In America, Ettore took on the name Hector Boyardee, and started building toward his dreams.

With a combination of skill, ambition, and lots of hard work, "Hector" eventually earned the position of head chef at the famous **Plaza Hotel** in New York City. As the head chef, he was responsible for feed-ing hundreds or thousands of people each week, and soon he gained a reputation for his delicious food. In 1915, Chef Boyardee was honored when he was chosen to cook for the wedding reception of **President Woodrow Wilson**.

Around that same time, Chef Boyardee achieved one of his lifelong goals by open-ing his very own restaurant named Giardino d'Italia in Cleveland, Ohio. The restaurant was an immediate success, and soon the chef had a loyal following of customers. These customers loved his food so much

that eventually Chef Boyardee began mak-ing pre-packaged versions.

When World War II began, the United States government asked the chef to help make food for soldiers overseas. This gave the Chef Boyardee brand a huge financial boost, and the company quickly grew into one of the biggest of its kind in the entire country. Many years later, when Ettore was ready to retire from the business, he agreed to sell it to a company called American Home Foods for almost $6 million.

Today, Chef Boyardee is still a beloved name to children throughout America, and Ettore Boiardi is remembered as one of America's many success stories.

A largely self-taught and peerlessly driven **photojournalist**, **ALFRED EISENSTAEDT**'s dedication and drive helped him to become one of the single most respected and revered professionals in the history of his field.

Eisenstaedt was born in 1898 in what is now Poland, and his early life resembled that of many young men in Germany during the early 1900s. A student at the University of Berlin who went on the serve in the German Army during World War I, the young Eisenstaedt worked quietly as a belt salesman in the years immediately following the war. During this time, he taught himself the art of photography, eventually finding work as a freelance photojournalist. In 1929, almost a decade after the end of the war, Eisenstaedt got his first big break when he was hired to cover the **Nobel Prize** ceremony that year in Stockholm. There, the young photojournalist began to distinguish himself as one of the most talented photographers of his generation, capturing the wonder and enormity of the events he was assigned to cover.

Following his work on the Nobel Prize ceremony, Eisenstaedt continued freelancing with various publications, even covering the rise of Adolf Hitler in post-World War I Germany. In 1935, after he had already established himself as one of the era's foremost photojournalists, he immigrated to the United States. In America, he worked with industry giants such as *Harper's Bazaar*, *Vogue*, and eventually *LIFE* magazine, which had just begun to publish.

At *LIFE,* Eisenstaedt found his true home, and today he is attributed as one of the driving forces behind the magazine's early success. His judgment and ability to capture moving photographs of any event helped to build the magazine's dedicated readership, who purchased it as much for its stunning imagery as for the articles they accompanied. Importantly, Alfred Eisenstaedt was one of several European photographers, who during the early and mid-twentieth century, brought their knowledge to the United States, adding to and deepening the growing culture of photography here.

By the end of his professional career, Eisenstaedt had spent more than four decades with *LIFE,* working well into his eighties. During that time, he photographed everything that one could imagine: royalty, the common people, celebrations and hardships, wartime and peace. Today, Alfred Eisenstaedt is remembered as a true pioneer in the field of photojournalism. He began his story as a young salesman in Berlin, who owned little more than a dream and the determination to pursue it.

One of the modern time's most revered and respected **filmmakers**, **ALFRED HITCHCOCK'S** work produced a long-lasting and hugely influential legacy which still exists today.

Born on August 13, 1899, in London, England, to very strict parents, Alfred Hitchcock often described a very harsh and lonely childhood, where he felt cut off from the world. As a young man, he attended St. Ignatius College in Enfield, England, before enrolling in art courses at the University of London. It was at that university where his love of film truly began to grow, and immediately after graduating from school, he began working in sales and later moved to the advertising department at W. T. Henley's Telegraph Works Company.

While working in advertising, Hitchcock pursued his own writing, creating countless short stories that he would submit to Henley's company publication. He found success in his stories containing twist endings and surprising plots, which were employed with great talent even in his earliest manuscripts.

In 1920, Hitchcock left the cable company to begin work with the Famous Players–Lasky Corporation, a film studio. There, Alfred designed title cards for the company's silent films and continued to work on his personal stories and skills. Soon, he worked his way up and moved from title card designer to assistant director, then from assistant director to full **director**.

In 1925, Alfred Hitchcock directed his very first film, and over the next several decades, he created countless movies with his classic suspenseful and twisted style. His early works, such as *Blackmail* and *The 39 Steps*, introduced viewers to the thrill of Hitchcock's storytelling, which was very different from most of the movies being made at that time.

Wanting bigger things, Hitchcock moved to Hollywood in 1939 and immediately began making films there. His first movie directed in the United States was called *Rebecca*, and it won him an **Academy Award**, cementing his reputation as one of his generation's finest filmmakers. Interestingly, Hitchcock enjoyed appearing in his own films in cameos, and many fans delighted in seeing the director.

Throughout his career, Hitchcock created and directed more than fifty movies, including the classics *Rear Window*, *Vertigo*, *North by Northwest*, and *Psycho*. He received countless awards from almost every notable film organization. Today, he is remembered as one of the founders of the **thriller** genre, and film fans today still love his works. Without Alfred Hitchcock, filmmaking would look very different today.

A successful entrepreneur, respected judge, and beloved **U.S. representative** in Southern California, **DALIP SINGH SAUND**, known simply as "**Judge**" by his friends and colleagues, lived a life of service and dedication to his community.

Born on September 20, 1899, in the British-controlled Indian province of Chhajjalwaddi, Saund's early life was marked by hardship and stacked odds. His father, a government-employed construction contractor, passed away when Saund was only a young boy. Despite this, he began his education at a very young age in a one-room schoolhouse, which had been started by his own father and uncles in order to provide Saund and other children with the schooling they were never afforded. This made a profound impact on Saund and he spent much of his life working tirelessly to support and improve the communities in which he lived.

At eight years old, the young Saund attended a boarding school near his home, and as a young man, he continued his education at the University of Punjab. During his time at university, Saund was a vocal advocate for Indian independence from British rule, and he mixed his courses in mathematics with the study of nonviolent civil disobedience. After his graduation in 1919, while waiting for clearance to immigrate to the United States, Saund worked tirelessly to improve the community in which he had grown up by planting trees, establishing banks, and expanding the school that his family had helped build.

After coming to the United States to pursue higher education, the young man found himself heavily influenced by America's belief in the power of freedom, and soon his plans to learn about agriculture had grown into a desire to build a better life for himself and people like him. Despite experiencing extreme bias and discrimination toward people of Asian descent—which was rampant during the early twentieth century in America—Saund's belief in the strength of the American dream persisted.

After earning his **doctorate**, Saund began his career as an entrepreneur, redefining what was possible for Asian Americans of his generation. Later, his drive for financial success would evolve into a dream for a better future for all minorities, and he began to advocate for legislation granting Indian immigrants the ability to earn full American citizenship. In 1952, after an intense election dominated by anti-Indian discrimination, Saund was elected as judge in Southern California—a position that he used to help refresh and support underrepresented communities.

In 1957, after another election campaign throughout which he faced discrimination and still he refused to attack his opponents, Saund was elected to **Congress** and became the first Asian American to ever possess full voting rights in the United States Congress. During his time as an elected official, Saund continued to serve his community and fought relentlessly for legislation that would support everyone—no matter their background.

An artist of immense personal talent and vision, **LOUISE NEVELSON'S** sculptures and dedication to her own unique style helped to shape the trends and nature of mid-twentieth-century American fine art.

Originally born as Louise Berliawsky on September 23, 1899, in what is now Ukraine, Louise Nevelson fled with her family to the United States when she was only a young girl to escape Russian discrimination against Jews. They settled in Rockland, Maine, where Nevelson soon discovered a budding love of art—specifically **sculpture**. After graduating from high school in Rockland and marrying a local entrepreneur, Nevelson and her husband moved to New York.

In New York, however, Nevelson's passion for art could no longer be denied, and she began studying at schools and organizations throughout the city despite her family's disapproval. In 1931, as her talent continued to grow, she left New York and her husband to study in Munich, Germany, at the Academy of Fine Arts. Only one year later, however, in 1932, her mentor and head of the school, Hans Hofmann, was forced to leave Germany to escape the growing Nazi power in the country. Because of this, Nevelson returned to the United States as a very different woman.

Back in the States, she devoted herself entirely to art, studying painting, sculpture, and even modern dance. Over the following decade, she would meet and be influenced by other twentieth-century art titans, such as Frida Kahlo and Diego Rivera, who helped inspire in Nevelson a love and fascination for **Central American imagery**.

In the 1940s, Nevelson began to cement her place as a truly influential artist of the mid-twentieth century despite the open and aggressive discrimination against female artists that was all too common during the era. Nonetheless, Nevelson persevered, continuing to produce the groundbreaking and unique sculptures that set her apart from her contemporaries. Unlike other her peers, who worked almost exclusively with traditional materials such as marble and metal, Nevelson worked with scrap wood.

During the height of her popularity, Nevelson's work heavily featured themes and imagery from her extensive travels through Central America. Today, Louise Nevelson is remembered as a truly original artist, who defied traditions and expectations in order to create her own art and vision, and in doing so, helped reimagine the future of modern art.

◆ **HYMAN G. RICKOVER** was an engineer, innovator, and military veteran who was one of the driving forces behind the development of the first-ever **nuclear-powered submarine** and other related technologies that shaped the twentieth century.

Born on January 27, 1900, as Chaim Godalia Rickover in the area of modern-day Poland, Rickover and his family immigrated to the United States when he was a young boy in order to escape anti-Jewish discrimination in Russia. Though the family first moved to New York City, they quickly relocated to Chicago, where they settled for much of his childhood. To help support his family, Rickover got his first job at only nine years old, and his strong work ethic continued for the rest of his life.

After graduating from high school, Rickover looked to the U.S. Naval Academy instead of college as it was much less expensive. He was accepted and immediately proved himself to be an excellent student, graduating in 1922 at the top of his class. Following his graduation, Rickover served on an American warship, where he quickly earned the rank of engineer officer for his reliability, work ethic, and intelligence.

After his duty aboard warships, Rickover returned to his education, eventually earning a master's degree in **electrical engineering**, an achievement that would help him advance even further within the navy. By 1939, Rickover had been promoted to assistant chief of the electrical section of the Bureau of Engineering, and during World War II, he headed the same section.

Perhaps his greatest contribution to American history, though, was his work on nuclear energy, which began after World War II. Inspired by a military project to construct a nuclear electric power plant, Rickover began advocating for the development of nuclear-powered submarines. While at first many of his superiors and fellow engineers did not think such an invention was possible, Rickover was convinced that his idea was valuable. After many years of campaigning for the creation of such a submarine, Rickover was finally promoted to director of the Nuclear Power Division, Bureau of Ships and was able to order construction of the submarine himself.

The ship, named the USS **Nautilus**, began construction in 1951, and by 1954, it was completed and christened. The *Nautilus* was a complete success, breaking numerous records for voyage duration and distance traveled, and today Hyman Rickover and the *Nautilus* are viewed as an important moment in the history of American technology.

During America's long history of on-stage theater and on film, few **directors** have been as influential or as important as **LEE STRASBERG**, who helped build the modern foundation of American theater in the early 1900s.

Born on November 17, 1901, in what is now Ukraine, Strasberg and his family immigrated to the United States when he was only seven years old and settled in New York City. There, the young Strasberg was exposed to American theater and quickly fell in love with it. Though he initially worked as an actor, his life was changed forever after he attended a play directed by **Konstantin Stanislavsky** in 1923. Inspired now to eventually become a director himself, Lee took a job with the Theatre Guild in New York and began to work as both an assistant stage manager and actor.

In 1929, after many years of supporting and exploring theater in New York City, Strasberg retired to focus full time on his goal of directing. In 1931, he began **the Group Theatre**, through which he would direct countless plays, eventually earning his first **Pulitzer Prize** for direction of the play *Men in White* by Sidney Kingsley.

Looking to share his knowledge, Strasberg joined the **Actors Studio** in 1948, where he worked as an acting teacher. Basing much of his teaching style off his idol Konstantin Stanislavsky, Strasberg quickly became one of the studio's most respected teachers, and students flocked to the organization to be taught by him. Specifically, Strasberg encouraged his students to use **method acting** to improve their skills, which meant that actors and actresses had to use experiences from their own lives to make their performances more believable. Though this was seen as extremely difficult, the method was soon adopted by many talented performers of the time.

In the 1950s, after several years as a teacher, Strasberg was appointed to the position of artistic director for the Actors Guild. He held that position for more than three decades, during which time he worked with some of the twentieth century's most famous actors, including James Dean, Jane Fonda, and Al Pacino.

Today, Lee Strasberg is revered as one of the most important founders of modern American theater. Countless performers, directors, and teachers remember him with utmost respect, carrying forward his legacy of excellence and dedication.

A most-cherished American comic, a giant in the field of entertainment, and a committed humanitarian, **BOB HOPE** is one of the most memorable figures in American **comedy**.

Originally born Leslie Townes Hope in London in 1903, "Bob" Hope moved with his family to the United States when he was six years old. Hope's father worked as a stonemason in Cleveland, Ohio, where Bob grew up. Because of the enormous size of his family, Bob began working at a very young age to help pay the bills, and this work ethic followed him for the rest of his life.

Hope's mother began teaching him how to sing from childhood. This training, combined with regular dance lessons, helped the young Hope begin performing at local **vaudeville** theaters with his girlfriend at the time. The experience made Bob fall even more deeply in love with the stage, and he quickly began seeking out other acts and partners with which he could expand his experience. By 1927, when Hope was only twenty-four, he found success with partner George Byrne and legendary film star Fatty Arbuckle. Together, the three worked together on *Sidewalks of New York*, a play that took Hope to the **Broadway** stage for the first time.

By the 1930s, Hope's career had truly begun to explode. He had multiple other Broadway roles under his belt and invaluable experience that would help him begin his comedy career in later years. In 1937, Bob became a regular radio personality, and his popularity grew as fans fell in love with his rapid-fire wit—a style he carried with him when he began acting in films the next year. Thus began Bob Hope's long career of hit comedy films and television specials.

A repeat host of the Academy Awards and other such award shows, Hope became a household name in the mid-twentieth century. Despite his stardom, he never forgot his community. A dedicated humanitarian who maintained lifelong support for American servicemen, specifically, Bob spent countless holidays and vacations entertaining troops stationed around the world, and his popularity with the military was stronger than perhaps any other group.

By the end of his life, Bob Hope had received numerous accolades and honorary degrees, including being knighted by the British crown in 1998 and receiving a Medal of the Arts from President Bill Clinton in 1995. One of the twentieth century's most-decorated and beloved figures, Bob Hope is remembered today as a comedian with a heart of gold.

Through a mixture of natural talent, hard work, and pure love of dance, **GEORGE BALANCHINE** made himself into one of the single most important people in the history of modern **ballet**.

Born on January 22, 1904, as Georgy Melitonovich Balanchivadze in St. Petersburg, Russia, Balanchine was the son of a composer. Because of this, he discovered a love for music very early on in his childhood, and he carried that love with him for the rest of his life. In 1914, when he was only ten years old, Balanchine was enrolled at the Mariinsky Theatre ballet school, where he began his formal education in dance. He was a student there until 1921, when he went on to study music and composition at the Petrograd Conservatory of Music.

In 1924, after Balanchine toured with the Soviet State Dancers ballet company throughout Germany, he met another dancer named Serge Diaghilev. After only a short while together, Balanchine became the choreographer for Serge's world-famous **Ballet Russes**. For the next several years, Balanchine traveled with the Russes and designed their dances under his simplified name. Because of their success and popularity, Balanchine's reputation grew until he was a well-known and highly respected name in the world of ballet.

After the Ballet Russes group broke apart in the early 1930s, Balanchine decided it was time to form his own group, and so he created the Les Ballets company in 1933. Balanchine's group was an immediate success, and after an early performance, he was asked by American dance expert Lincoln Kirstein if they could work together. Balanchine accepted, and for the next fifty years, Kirstein and Balanchine worked to create some of the greatest modern ballet performances ever seen.

In 1934, the pair founded the **School of American Ballet**, and one year later in 1935, they began the American Ballet (now New York City Ballet), which was the official company of the famous New York Metropolitan Opera.

For the rest of his life, Balanchine directed and choreographed hundreds of ballets, many of which are remembered today as some of the greatest of the twentieth century. He also worked with film producers on Hollywood movies, helped choreograph pieces for Broadway musicals, and worked closely with musical geniuses such as the composer Igor Stravinsky.

Today, many historians of dance argue that George Balanchine's career and nearly five hundred ballets helped shape modern ballet, and that without his influence, the world of dance would not be the same.

An **author, philosopher, and lecturer** whose ideas and books helped shape minds throughout the course of her life, **AYN RAND** was a truly unique woman.

Originally born as Alissa Zinovievna Rosenbaum on February 2, 1905, in St. Petersburg, Russia, Rand was the eldest daughter of a wealthy Jewish family. For most of her early childhood, Rand lived well. She attended good schools where she excelled due to her natural intelligence and curiosity. In 1917, however, with anti-Jewish discrimination rising in Russia, government forces seized the shop owned by Rand's family and forced them out of their home.

In 1924, when Rand was nineteen years old, she graduated from the Leningrad State University and immediately continued her education, enrolling in the State Institute for Cinematography. Surprisingly, Rand studied screenwriting during this time, even though her focus would later turn to novels and philosophy.

After obtaining a visa, Rand immigrated to Chicago in 1926 and lived there with extended family for a couple of months before moving on. She changed her name to Ayn Rand and next found herself in Hollywood, where she could pursue her dream of becoming a screenwriter for American films. Eventually, she earned a job as a clerk at RKO Radio Pictures, a film studio, and through hard work and determination, Rand climbed the professional ladder there. Working as head of wardrobe, she continued writing screenplays on her own time, and in 1932, Rand sold *Red Pawn* to Universal Studios.

In 1934, after she had written and sold a few other screenplays, Rand and her husband moved to New York City. There, her career as an author began to grow when she published her first novel, *We the Living*. Finding a new love for novels, Rand continued to write, and despite many rejections from publishing houses, she eventually completed one of her most popular works, **The Fountainhead**. This finally earned her the public attention and success she deserved, and a few years later, *The Fountainhead* was adapted into a feature film.

Over the next several decades, Rand continued to develop her style and beliefs, eventually writing what would become perhaps the most popular book of her career, **Atlas Shrugged.** Although the book contained controversial beliefs and philosophy, it was a massive commercial success and loved by her readers. Later, Rand developed the themes of her works into a branch of philosophy she coined **objectivism**, which gained support with fans of her work. For the last several decades of her career, Rand focused almost entirely on writing articles and essays about her philosophy.

Though a controversial figure, Ayn Rand forever left her mark on the world and on Western literature. Her writing remains important today, prompting healthy discussion and debate between fans and writers.

A Swedish American **starlet** who graced both silent and "talkie" movie screens in the years before World War II, **GRETA GARBO** was a mysterious actress who quickly found popularity and fame with American audiences.

Originally born Greta Lovisa Gustafsson on September 18, 1905, in Stockholm, Sweden, Garbo's early childhood was marked by poverty and personal struggles. Her father, who worked as a laborer in Stockholm, was in extremely poor health, and by the time she turned thirteen years old, Garbo had to drop out of school to care for him. He passed away two years later, and his death greatly affected the young girl.

Soon, Garbo found a job promoting men's clothing at a Swedish department store, where she discovered her natural talent and passion for film. By 1922, she had already starred in a small comedy film called *Peter the Tramp*, and her work quickly gained recognition in the Swedish film industry. A short time later, Garbo received a scholarship to Sweden's Royal Dramatic Theatre, a respected school for young actors. She only studied for a year, however, before leaving school to star in *The Legend of Gosta Berling* under director Mauritz Stiller, who gave her the surname Garbo.

The film was a massive hit, and Garbo instantly became a recognized face. Over the next several years, she continued working with Stiller, and together they formed a strong reputation in the film industry. In 1925, however, when Garbo was only nineteen years old, she moved to the United States to expand her career. Soon, she was hired by **MGM** and began starring in some of their biggest movies, such as *The Temptress*. The films were immediate successes, earning enormous popularity for Garbo and huge profits for the studio, who valued her highly.

For Garbo, who remembered her impoverished childhood, the goal was to have complete control of her own money. Because of this, she negotiated a groundbreaking contract with MGM that granted her near total power over her roles.

Greta Garbo's combination of beauty, talent, and confidence mixed with her mysterious nature made her one of America's most beloved movie stars in the early 1900s. In addition, her willingness to fight for her rights helped reform the film industry. Today, she is remembered as one of the most famous movie starlets of the pre-World War II era, and her influence persists today.

◆ **BILLY WILDER**, originally named Samuel Wilder, was an Austrian-born film **director** and **producer** who charmed his viewers with funny, sarcastic commentary on the world and American life.

Born on June 22, 1906, in what is now Poland, Samuel Wilder was nicknamed "Billy" by his mother, who had spent several years in the United States as a young girl. There, she fell in love with the story of "Buffalo Bill," the American hero, and many years later used his name for her son.

As a child, Billy was raised in the city of Vienna, and he attended school there. As a young man, he enrolled at the University of Vienna to study law but dropped out after only one year in order to work as a sports reporter for a local newspaper. In 1926, after he had spent some time working for the paper, he was offered a job by a large Berlin-based newspaper, where he covered stories about crime.

In 1929, Billy found his first success with film and began working on the German movie *People on Sunday*. Following the film's release, Wilder continued living and writing in Germany until he was forced to leave the country due to the rise of the Nazis. Though he moved to France initially, Billy Wilder eventually immigrated to the United States and settled in Hollywood in 1933. Despite having very little money and speaking almost no English, Billy worked hard in his new home.

After more than four years of dedication and effort, Wilder got his first big break when he met fellow film professional Charles Brackett in 1938. The pair began a working relationship and friendship which lasted more than twelve years, and together they created several box-office hits such as **Sunset Boulevard** and **Hold Back the Dawn**. Many of the films used Wilder's background as a crime reporter in order to make their stories feel more real and suspenseful. Because of this, Wilder and Brackett's films earned a large and devoted fan base.

For the next several decades, Billy Wilder was one of the biggest names in American film. His movies, although mostly suspense and crime-focused, also branched out into comedies and thoughtful commentary on life in America. Though widely successful, many of Wilder's films were considered controversial for the real-life topics they contained.

By the end of his life and career, Billy Wilder had established himself as one of the most influential directors and filmmakers of the twentieth century. He has since been honored with awards including the National Medal of Arts, which was given to him by President Bill Clinton.

◆ **HANNAH ARENDT** was a **humanitarian**, **political thinker**, and gifted **speaker** who fought bravely for justice and the rights of people all around the world.

Born on October 14, 1906, in Hanover, Germany, Arendt's early childhood was marked by tragedy. When she was only seven years old, her father passed away, and Hannah's mother was left to raise her. The young Hannah, however, proved to be a brilliant and tough child. In school, her natural intelligence and work ethic set her apart as an excellent student.

As a young woman, Arendt enrolled in the University of Marburg, where she studied philosophy and ethics. In 1929, at the University of Heidelberg, Arendt earned her doctoral degree under Professor Karl Jaspers. The two would remain friends for the rest of their lives, and they often shared conversations about the nature of ethics and philosophy.

Only four short years later, however, in 1933, Hannah Arendt was forced to flee Germany as the Nazis rose to power. Though she lived temporarily in the Czech Republic, Hannah soon moved to Paris. From there, she worked tirelessly with the Youth Aliyah organization, helping to rescue young Jewish people from Nazi-controlled territory.

After Nazi Germany gained control of France, Arendt was imprisoned in a concentration camp. She could not be held, however, and escaped in the early 1940s. Following her escape, Hannah fled Europe and settled in New York. While in America, Arendt wrote countless essays and articles about **human rights** and the horrors of anti-Semitism. She quickly became one of the leading humanitarian voices during World War II and was never afraid to speak out against injustice and evil.

In the 1950s, Hannah Arendt began publishing longer books that detailed the rise of the Nazis and specifically how the party came to be created. Arendt's other books were intelligent, thoughtful works on the nature of democracy and political freedom, arguing that constitutional democracy, like that of America, was essential for a fair and just society.

Later, Hannah became a professor at universities throughout America. Teaching at Princeton, the University of Chicago, Berkeley, and others, she helped shape young minds and create a kinder, more thoughtful generation of thinkers. Today, she is remembered for her legacy of deep thinking, compassion, and fierce spirit that saw her fight through some of the darkest times in modern history.

One of modern history's most brilliant scientists and **nuclear physicists, EDWARD TELLER'S** work on the creation of the atom bomb helped to shape the world into what it is today.

Born on January 15, 1908, in Budapest, Hungary, to a wealthy Jewish family, Edward was a hard-working and brilliant student. His dedication to education started early in his hometown of Budapest. This dedication continued when, in 1927, he earned a degree in chemical engineering from the Institute of Technology in Karlsruhe, Germany, when he was only nineteen years old. Only three years later, in 1930, Teller received his doctoral degree in physics from the University of Leipzig.

Edward Teller's journey was only just beginning. Following his graduation, Teller began research on atomic physics, the subject that would define the rest of his career. Edward worked as a professor in Europe for many years until, in 1935, he traveled with his wife to the United States to teach at George Washington University.

Then, in 1939, Teller's life changed forever after fellow scientist Niels Bohr released his research on nuclear fission. This, combined with a speech by President Franklin D. Roosevelt calling for all scientists to aid the United States against the Nazis, spurred Teller into action. Almost immediately, he began exploring how his research into nuclear physics might be used to make **weapons**.

In 1941, Teller worked with a team of scientists at the University of Chicago to create the first nuclear chain reaction. This success earned him an invitation to work with famous scientist J. Robert Oppenheimer at a secret laboratory in New Mexico. There, Teller would work with a team of scientists on what was known as the **Manhattan Project**.

For many years, the team worked tireless to create the world's first fission bomb.

When the bomb was eventually completed and used, however, many of the scientists who had worked on it lost interest in the technology. They, including Edward Teller, believed that the destruction caused by the weapon was too great, and that creating it had been a mistake. Despite this, Teller resumed his work for the U.S. government in 1946 as a consultant. In that position, he helped to guide their research into the creation of a new type of thermonuclear weapon, the **hydrogen bomb**.

Though a controversial figure, Edward Teller propelled modern technology to new heights. Today, he is remembered not only as the "father" of the hydrogen bomb but also as a brilliant creator who explored the mysteries of nuclear energy.

JOHN KENNETH GALBRAITH was an **economist**, **writer**, and **government adviser** who fought tirelessly for fair and just policies to help the American people.

Born on October 15, 1908, in Ontario, Canada, John Kenneth Galbraith was raised by his father, who worked as a farmer and schoolteacher, and his mother, who was a homemaker and activist. His early childhood was shaped by his parents' involvement in the United Farmers of Ontario organization, which helped protect farmers and their families. Because of this, John believed early on that the government and its laws should help protect everyone and not only the people at the top.

Though he attended a small, one-room school as a boy, Galbraith went on to earn his bachelor's degree from the Ontario Agricultural College. He was such a devoted and intelligent student that he was awarded a scholarship, which allowed him to move to Berkeley, California. There, he studied and received his master's degree and doctoral degree from the University of California. While at school in California, Galbraith became interested in the field of **economics**, and soon began to write and publish papers on the topic.

Starting in 1934, Galbraith taught at Harvard University, and in 1937, he officially became a U.S. citizen. For many years after, he traveled to teach and learn while he developed his own beliefs about economics and social justice. Unlike many academics who avoided political life, Galbraith willingly served as an adviser for many government boards and committees. He hoped that, by doing so, he could help to build a better American economy to protect and serve every citizen.

After World War II, Galbraith was hired to a senior position in the **U.S. Department of**

State, where he was responsible for economic policy with many foreign countries. While in that position, he tried to change many aspects of the government, but was met with distrust and resistance by other career politicians. Though he did his best to reform what he saw as outdated beliefs in the government, he eventually resigned and returned to writing articles and essays about economics.

Throughout his career, John Kenneth Galbraith was a brave and outspoken defender of the common people. Unlike many economists, who focused on large companies and the rich, John believed that the best economy was one that treated everyone well and allowed them to live a good life. Today, many of his beliefs are still used by liberal activists who argue that the American economy should be reformed.

RITA LEVI-MONTALCINI, the Italian-born **neurologist** and scientist, advanced our understanding of the human brain perhaps more than any other researcher in history.

Born on April 22, 1909, in Turin, Italy, Rita was the youngest of four children in a wealthy and loving Jewish family. Her father, Adamo, was a respected mathematician and electrical engineer. Rita's mother, Adele, was a painter and humanitarian. Rita herself grew up surrounded by art, science, and love, flourishing into an intelligent and curious young woman. Though she was raised in a traditional, conservative setting where women were supposed to be caretakers and homemakers, Rita broke from tradition in early adulthood.

At twenty years old, Rita Levi-Montalcini enrolled at the University of Turin where she began studying medicine. There, she made lifelong friendships with fellow scientists Salvador Luria and Renato Dulbecco, who shared Rita's curiosity and passion for learning.

In 1936, when Rita was twenty-seven, she graduated from medical school and began her education in neurology and psychiatry. She had always had an interest in the **human brain**, and she began her career exploring its mysteries. That same year, however, the Italian government signed laws discriminating against Jews and other so-called non-Aryan Italians, and Rita was forced to leave her home country. After spending a short time in Brussels, where she worked at a neurological academy, Rita eventually returned to Turin. She reunited with her family and decided to continue her research privately, at home.

In 1941, World War II had become increasingly violent in the areas near Turin. In order to escape constant bombing, Rita fled with her family to Florence, where they lived underground until World War II ended. In 1944, Rita worked as a doctor at a refugee camp, treating deadly diseases every day.

After the war's official end in 1945, Rita was invited to travel to St. Louis to help Professor Viktor Hamburger with his research. Although Rita had only planned to stay in America for about a year, she soon become fascinated by the research and stayed for more than thirty years.

That research, combined with Rita's own work into **nerve cells** and the human brain, won her international acclaim among scientists. Countless papers, experiments, and books have been written because of her work on the human brain. In 1986, Rita was awarded the **Nobel Prize for Physiology or Medicine**, and one year later, she was awarded the National Medal of Science. Today, she is remembered as a woman who braved some of history's darkest years to expand our understanding of the human brain.

◆ **ELIA KAZAN** was an enormously talented **author** and **director** who worked during the early twentieth century to help develop modern American theater into what it is today.

Born on September 7, 1909, as Elia Kazanjoglous in Constantinople (now Istanbul, Turkey) to a Greek family, Elia immigrated to the United States when he was only four years old. There, his family settled in New York City, where his father opened a business as a rug salesman. As a young boy, Elia attended school in the city, where he was exposed to New York's long tradition of **theater**. Following high school, Kazan enrolled at Williams College in Massachusetts, and then he began his lifelong career in the theater when he began his advanced studies in drama at Yale University.

In the early and mid-1930s, Elia Kazan was part of the Group Theatre in New York, which specialized in experimental techniques. There, Kazan learned **method acting,** which he would employ for much of his career. These techniques involved an actor remembering true experiences or emotions in order to make their performances more realistic.

Once the Group Theatre disbanded in 1941, Kazan changed the focus of his career from acting to directing. Almost immediately, Kazan's work as a director earned him praise around New York, and in the following years, he even began working on Hollywood films. His movies, which included classics such as *A Tree Grows in Brooklyn* and *Gentleman's Agreement,* brought him great success and a strong reputation in the theater industry. Importantly, many of his works tackled difficult subjects such as anti-Semitism and interracial marriage, which many directors shied away from at the time.

Perhaps one of Kazan's greatest successes came in 1947, with the play *A Streetcar Named Desire* by Tennessee Williams. This play was a massive hit and is often credited for truly launching the career of iconic actor Marlon Brando. Following the play's success, Elia Kazan and Marlon Brando worked together for another decade. In 1954, Kazan's film *On the Waterfront*, starring Brando, won each of them an **Oscar** for their work.

Kazan's career continued to earn one success after another both on stage and in film, and in the later decades of his life, he even wrote several successful novels. In 1999, he was awarded a Lifetime Achievement Oscar, only one of many awards he earned throughout his career. Today, he is remembered as an important and influential piece of the history of modern American theater.

One of the most multitalented, intelligent, creative, and graceful people of the twentieth century, **HEDY LAMARR** was a woman who defied all expectations. From **actress** to **inventor**, Lamarr's accomplishments make her one of the most impressive people in American history.

Born on November 9, 1914, as Hedwig Eva Maria Kiesler in Vienna, Austria, to a wealthy Jewish family, Hedy's natural curiosity was encouraged early in life by her father. As a young girl, Hedy and her father would walk around the city's streets as he answered every question she could think of. While Lamarr's father encouraged the inventive and scientific part of her mind, Lamarr's mother focused on building her appreciation for the arts. Her mother, who was a concert pianist, enrolled young Hedy in both ballet and piano, and she excelled at both.

By sixteen years of age, however, the world had begun focusing more on Hedy's beauty than her intelligence. She was recruited by theater director Max Reinhardt to begin studying acting in Berlin, Germany, and that year, in 1930, she gave her first performance in the German film *Money on the Street*. Over the next several years, Lamarr appeared in many films as her reputation grew.

In 1933, she married an Austrian munitions manufacturer named Fritz Mandl who first learned of Hedy through her films. She was very unhappy in the marriage, though, and in 1937, she escaped her husband by moving to London. There, she met the film producer Louis B. Mayer, who worked for MGM in Hollywood. After she immigrated to Hollywood, Hedy quickly became as famous in American movies as she was in European films.

Not content to simply be a pretty face or beloved actress, Hedy pursued her passion for **engineering** and invention while in Hollywood. Though Hedy invented many things such as new kinds of traffic lights, her most impressive invention came in the years before World War II. Working with composer George Antheil, who she had met at a dinner party, Hedy developed a new type of **communication system**. This new device prevented messages from being intercepted by enemy forces.

Although Hedy Lamarr's genius was not widely recognized during her lifetime, history remembers her as a woman of impressive intelligence. In 1997, only three years before her death, she was given the Pioneer Award for her work on the radio device, and in 2014, she was inducted into the National Inventors Hall of Fame. Today, many remember her as **"the mother of Wi-Fi"** because of how her discoveries helped to create modern-day technologies like that found in our phones and computers.

ANTHONY RUDOLPH OAXACA QUINN was a Mexican-born **actor** whose work in beloved plays and films made him one of the most celebrated performers of the mid-twentieth century.

Born on April 21, 1915, in Chihuahua, Mexico, Anthony and his family moved to Los Angeles, California, when he was very young. Tragically, Anthony's father died when Anthony was only nine years old. As a young boy, however, Anthony began working whatever jobs he could to help his family pay the bills. Despite working so much and at such a young age, Anthony still excelled in his studies.

When in high school, Anthony received first place in an architecture competition, which won him the opportunity to be mentored by architectural legend Frank Lloyd Wright. Wright asked Anthony to enroll at an acting school just so that he could learn to speak more confidently. But while at acting school, Anthony discovered his lifelong love for the **theater**.

By 1936, Anthony had fully devoted himself to acting, performing alongside fellow American icon Mae West in the play *Clean Beds*. Over the next several decades, Anthony's reputation and skill grew until he was ranked among the finest actors of his generation. Between 1950 and 1962, Quinn acted in scores of films and plays, and he racked up an impressive number of awards and honors for his work. Whether it was Broadway or the big screen, his charm and talent earned him a devoted fanbase.

Specifically, Anthony Quinn was known for playing characters such as Mexican revolutionaries or even Zeus, the Greek god. In many of his most popular films and plays, he played the villain because of his brooding good looks.

Though Quinn performed in more than two hundred films, his interests turned to other types of art as time passed. During the 1980s and onward, he began exploring other passions such as painting, sculpting, jewelry designing, and even book writing. By the end of his life in 2001, Anthony Quinn enjoyed a steady stream of accolades, such as a **Tony** nomination, two **Academy Awards** for Best Supporting Actor, and a **Foreign Language Oscar**.

Today, Anthony Quinn is remembered as one of the most recognizable and skilled Mexican American actors of the early and mid-twentieth century. His work in film and on the stage has helped to inspire many actors of Mexican heritage, and his legacy helped shape modern American theater.

ELIZABETH STERN was a Canadian-born **scientist** whose research into the development of cancer in the human body has helped save countless patients in the twentieth and twenty-first centuries.

Born on September 19, 1915, in Ontario, Canada, Elizabeth was the daughter of Polish immigrants who had fled Eastern Europe to escape anti-Jewish discrimination. A bright and dedicated student, Elizabeth performed brilliantly in school. By the time she was twenty-three years old in 1939, she had graduated from the University of Toronto School of Medicine. During her time there, she met Solomon Shankman, a chemistry student and the man whom she would eventually marry.

After she married Solomon, Elizabeth moved to Los Angeles, California, where she continued her education at Cedars of Lebanon and the Good Samaritan hospitals. Specifically, Elizabeth focused on **pathology**, which studies the ways that different diseases affect the body.

In the decade between 1950 and 1960, Elizabeth Stern served as the director of research at the Los Angeles Cancer Detection Center, further exploring the way that **cancer** developed in human bodies. Although Stern's specific type of research was brand new and many scientists did not believe it was worth their effort, Stern was convinced that it was important. She ignored the disbelief and instead developed countless studies into **cryptopathology**.

Amazingly, Stern started to prove that she could predict cancer in patients by looking at certain key, early symptoms. This discovery shook the medical world. Even today, more than fifty years after Elizabeth Stern's research, scientists still use her work to predict and treat cancer.

Not yet done with her discoveries, Stern went on to develop the **Pap test**, which used computers and a special kind of procedure to predict cervical cancer earlier than any other test. The Pap test is still used today by doctors and hospitals all around the world.

Throughout her career, Elizabeth Stern faced constant doubt from those who could not understand her brilliant research—and often because she was a woman. Nonetheless, she never abandoned her ideals or passion. Because of her bravery and commitment to science, Elizabeth forever made the world a better, safer place.

Although she passed away in 1980 from stomach cancer, she is remembered today as one of the most important scientists of the twentieth century, and countless cancer patients have been protected by her genius. Without Elizabeth Stern, much medical technology we have today would not exist.

One of the single most respected and talented modern **architects, I. M. PEI** designed many of the most recognizable buildings of the twentieth century. His work continues to inspire architects and artists around the world.

Born on April 26, 1917, in Guangzhou, China, Ieoh Ming Pei spent almost his entire childhood in China. In 1935, however, when Pei was seventeen years old, he traveled to the United States to begin his education at the University of Pennsylvania, Philadelphia. After only a short time in Philadelphia, Pei transferred to the Massachusetts Institute of Technology (MIT), where he studied architectural engineering. Although he graduated from MIT in 1939, he was not allowed to return to China because of the events of World War II.

Instead, Pei remained in the United States and began taking contracts in New York City, Los Angeles, and Boston. The beginning of a long and impressive career, these early buildings showed hints of Pei's budding and remarkable style.

During World War II, Pei was recruited by the U.S. government to work with the National Defense Research Committee. This group researched all subjects that were potentially useful to the military, and Pei contributed his brilliant architecture mind to their work.

In 1945, Pei was hired as an assistant professor of design at Harvard University. He taught while earning his master's degree, which he completed in 1946.

In 1954, after Asian Americans were finally allowed to attain U.S. citizenship, Pei officially became a U.S. citizen. Only one year later, in 1955, he opened his own architecture firm named I. M. Pei & Associates and began creating his most recognizable buildings. One of his firm's very first buildings, named the **Mile High Center** in Denver, Colorado, earned him much publicity and respect in the world of architecture. Also committed to improving his community and those like it around the United States, Pei worked to design urban-renewal plans for cities along America's East Coast.

Over the next several decades, Pei would be hired to design and build some of America's most iconic structures. After the death of President John F. Kennedy, he was hired by Jacqueline Kennedy and the U.S. government to create a **presidential library** in the late president's honor. Constructed in Dorchester, Massachusetts, the library was finished in 1979, and Pei added onto it again a few years later.

Pei's most famous work was arguably completed in the 1980s, when he was hired to work on the **Louvre Museum** in Paris, France, and he created the iconic metal and glass pyramid in the square outside. Although controversial at first, it has since become one of the most popular architectural designs of the twentieth century.

One of the single most influential contemporary architects, I. M. Pei left a legacy of excellence, creativity, and unstoppable work ethic.

MAYA DEREN, originally known as Eleanora Derenkowsky, was a Ukrainian American **director** whose unique, experimental style helped to push American film into a new age of style.

Born on April 29, 1917, in Kiev, Ukraine, Maya was only five years old when her family immigrated to the United States in order to escape political unrest and anti-Semitism. Though her family found their new home in Syracuse, New York, they later moved to Ohio while Maya's father finished his degree in medicine at Syracuse University.

While Maya attended primary school in schools around the Syracuse area, in 1930, she traveled to Geneva, Switzerland, to study writing at the League of Nations School. After graduating in 1933, Maya returned to New York to continue studying journalism and political science.

During her education in Syracuse, she met Gregory Bardacke, who she eventually married. Following graduation, the two became active union organizers and community activists until 1938, when Maya divorced Bardacke. She earned her master's degree in English literature one year later.

Although she is known as a groundbreaking filmmaker, Maya Deren also pursued a wide range of other interests such as dance, poetry, and photography. During her lifetime, Maya published essays, worked with renowned photographers, and was active in political movements. Her passion for art and expression could not be contained by one medium.

In 1943, Maya completed her first **experimental film** titled *Meshes of the Afternoon*. A highly unique and strange movie, the work struggled to find mainstream success. Undeterred, Maya continued to create films over the next two decades. In the 1940s, she moved to New

York City and helped lay the foundation for American independent film.

Unable to find any large companies willing to promote her films and the films of other independent directors, Maya decided to do the job herself. She rented a theater in Greenwich Village in New York City, where she showed her own films and helped support other artists. Eventually she began an organization called the Creative Film Foundation to offer money and prizes to experimental filmmakers.

Though Maya Deren continued to make unique films, she tragically died in 1961 at the age of forty-four. Still, she left a legacy of avant-garde beauty, which helped develop the popular independent film industry of the twentieth and twenty-first centuries. Today, she is regarded as one of the most important figures in the history of independent film.

One of the single most recognizable and popular **chefs** of the twentieth century, **JOYCE CHEN** helped bring Chinese cuisine into mainstream American life. With her trademark charm and warm, welcoming personality, Chen introduced millions of Americans to a whole new world of food.

Born on September 12, 1917, as Liao Chia-ai in Beijing, China to a wealthy family, Chen began cooking as a young girl. Though Chen's father, a successful businessperson, hired a personal chef to cook the family's meals, young Joyce was fascinated by the kitchen. She learned many of her early skills and techniques simply from watching the personal chef prepare meals. Though she lacked formal training, Joyce Chen's natural talent and curiosity helped her become a skilled chef before she reached adulthood.

At eighteen years old, Chen planned, organized, and cooked her first professional dinner. It was a massive success and encouraged her to continue in culinary arts. Though she continued learning and cooking in China for some time, the Chinese Communist Revolution forced Chen and her family to flee. In 1949, the Chen family immigrated to the United States where they found a new home in Cambridge, Massachusetts.

Fortunately, Chen's new home was close to both Harvard University and MIT. Both universities had large populations of Chinese students, and Chen quickly realized that the students craved the food of their home country. Chen's skillful and **authentic Chinese dishes** were exactly what they wanted, and soon she had a strong reputation as a talented Chinese chef.

In 1958, Chen opened her very first restaurant, serving both Chinese and American dishes in large buffets. The restaurant was a roaring success, and a few years later, she began writing and publishing her own Chinese American **cookbooks**. In these cookbooks, Chen taught the reader how to make classic Chinese dishes and about chopsticks, tea ceremony, and the history of Chinese culinary traditions.

Almost a decade later in 1967, Chen opened her second restaurant. That same year, she hosted her own **cooking show** on Public Broadcasting Service (PBS). The show was filmed in the same studio as famous chef Julia Child, and the two eventually met and became great friends.

Over the course of her career and life, Joyce Chen promoted not only Chinese food but also Chinese culture. This was especially important because, for much of Chen's early time in America, Asian communities experienced frequent discrimination. Through her food and her love, Chef Chen broke down barriers and made America a better place, united through food.

ISAAC ASIMOV, born Isaak Yudovick Ozimov, was one of the twentieth century's most beloved and influential **science fiction writers**. His stories, which explored both science and human nature, were wonderful works of art that have helped inspired countless writers in the years since they were written.

Born on January 2, 1920, in Petrovichi, Russia, Asimov's family immigrated to the United States when he was only three years old. The family settled in Brooklyn, New York, and began their new life. Isaac's father, Judah, ran a local candy shop where he often had his young son work. A very intelligent child, Isaac taught himself to read before he was five years old. A decade later, when he was only fifteen, Isaac graduated from high school and went on to enroll at Columbia University.

At Columbia, the very young Asimov studied the sciences, eventually earning his bachelor's degree in 1939. By 1948, he had earned his doctorate degree from Columbia in chemistry. Still only twenty-eight years old, Asimov finally left his alma mater, where he had spent almost a third of his life. He immediately accepted a teaching position at Boston University's School of Medicine in 1949, and six years later, he was promoted to the position of associate professor of **biochemistry**.

As he grew older, however, his interest in teaching began to fade. Instead, his love of writing and stories became his new focus. Though he had published his first short story, **"Marooned Off Vesta,"** in 1938, it was not until 1950 that he had successfully published his first science fiction **novel**. From there, however, his passion continued to grow. Over the course of the next several years he produced and published an incredible number of short stories and books. Not limiting himself to science fiction, Asimov wrote on topics such as religion, astronomy, and math.

Throughout his career, Asimov wrote almost constantly. It is said that by the time of his passing in 1992, Isaac Asimov had written nearly five hundred books. Despite the sheer number of works, however, the quality of Isaac's writing was always impressive. During his career, Isaac was the winner of numerous honors and awards, including highly prized recognitions such as the **Hugo Award** and **Nebula Award**. With very few equals in the world of twentieth century science fiction writing, Isaac Asimov is remembered as one of the most influential and important writers in modern history. His books and legacy have inspired countless authors and creators, and his name will be remembered for many generations to come.

AN WANG was an **entrepreneur, engineer,** and **physicist** who helped create a new generation of computer technology. His contributions to manufacturing and computers lead to the invention of many devices we enjoy today.

Born on February 7, 1920, in Shanghai, China, Wang was the son of a professor who encouraged his son's appreciation of education and the sciences. For his entire childhood and much of his early adult life, An Wang lived and studied in China. In 1940, he earned his bachelor's degree in science from the Chiao-t'ung University in his home city. After graduation, Wang worked for the Chinese government developing radio technology to help China in a war against Japan. In return for his service, the Chinese government awarded Wang money to continue his education. Five years after graduating with his first degree in 1945, he immigrated to the United States to pursue higher education opportunities.

His path took him to Harvard University, where Wang began studying engineering and applied physics. Only three years after immigrating to the United States, Wang earned his doctoral degree from one of America's most respected universities. While at Harvard, Wang was exposed to some of the earliest **computer technology** for the first time, and he was fascinated by the devices. In 1948, the same year he graduated from Harvard, he invented the world's first magnetic memory core. This device was vital to the creation of better computer memories and was used until the microchip was created nearly a decade later.

In 1951, after his reputation as a leading inventor in computer science had continued to grow, An Wang began his own company named Wang Laboratories. The company manufactured various types of computers, including **desktop calculators**, and was highly successful over the next several decades. Eventually, in 1986, An Wang handed over the company to his son Frederick, but he returned in 1989 to lead the company once again as it fought to compete with fellow computing giant IBM.

Throughout his lifetime, An Wang's brilliance and work ethic set him apart as one of the single most successful Asian Americans of the twentieth century. By the time of his death in 1990, he had successfully obtained patents for more than forty of his inventions. Many of these helped inspire modern technology in the twenty-first century. Without An Wang's creative spirit and relentless dedication to the field of computer technology, our world would undoubtedly look very different today.

PAMELA HARRIMAN was a graceful and well-spoken woman, whose talent for diplomacy and persuasion helped her to become a respected **diplomat** and **social activist** during her lifetime.

Born on March 20, 1920, in Hampshire, England, Harriman was minor royalty. Her father, Baron Edward Digby of Hampshire, invested heavily in his daughter, and thanks to this, Pamela received high-quality education from hired tutors and governesses.

Among her many skills, Pamela had an impressive talent for horseback riding. Throughout her childhood and young adulthood, Harriman competed in many horseback riding competitions across her home country.

Pamela's education took her everywhere, with the young woman attending boarding school in Munich at seventeen before going on to Paris, where she took classes at the Sorbonne, the second oldest college in Europe.

In 1939, when she was working as a French-to-English translator at the Foreign Office in London, Pamela Harriman met Randolph Churchill. Randolph, the son of famous World War II-era Prime Minister Winston Churchill, proposed to Pamela on the night they met. Though they would eventually divorce, Pamela's marriage to Churchill helped expose her to the innerworkings of government. For the rest of her life, Harriman would maintain an eager interest in political matters.

In the 1950s Harriman immigrated to the United States, where she met Averell Harriman. Averell, who was a former governor of New York, helped further Pamela's education in politics. While they were married, Pamela often traveled with Averell to meet foreign leaders and sat in on their conversations.

After she obtained U.S. citizenship in the 1980s, Pamela began to work as a **political activist**. She founded Democrats for the '80s, a group devoted to world peace and healthy foreign affairs. She is credited with being one of the first to introduce Bill Clinton to Washington, back when he was only the governor of Arkansas.

Throughout her career, Pamela served in many positions. She was named a trustee of Rockefeller University, served as a U.S. ambassador to France, and co-chaired the Bill Clinton and Al Gore presidential campaign.

Though she started from a place of privilege, Pamela Harriman's intelligence, charm, and focus shaped her into an important player in twentieth-century politics. Her life was one filled with adventure, and she traveled the world as the writer of her own story.

ISAAC STERN, a Russian American artist who spent much of his life in the United States, was a uniquely gifted **musician** who rose to popularity for his emotional and beautiful musical performances.

Born on July 21, 1920, in what is now Ukraine, Isaac and his family immigrated to the United States when he was only one year old. They found a home in San Francisco, California, and began their new life. When he was six years old, Isaac's parents introduced him to piano lessons. He showed great potential for the instrument, but by the time he turned ten, Isaac had switched his focus to the **violin**.

A musical prodigy, the young Stern studied at the San Francisco Conservatory between the ages of eight and eleven. When he was twelve, Isaac begun studying under his mentor, Russian violinist Naoum Blinder. At only fifteen years of age, Isaac debuted with the San Francisco Symphony.

From there, Isaac's career continued to grow by leaps and bounds. By the time he was a young adult, he had already drawn national attention for his emotional, expressive style. He began touring Europe, playing to large crowds at elaborate festivals worldwide. So great was his talent that he was asked by many composers to premiere their new works, meaning that he was the first to play them in public.

In 1960, Isaac Stern began playing with friends and fellow musicians like pianist Eugene Istomin and cellist Leonard Rose. Together, the three toured and performed a series of concerts in honor of composer Ludwig van Beethoven's bicentennial.

Stern was also actively involved with his fans and the public. Throughout his career, he was known to appear on radio and television shows to talk about his performances and music in general. Additionally, Isaac was very active within many arts programs and organizations intended to support the musical arts. In 1960, Isaac was one of the primary reasons that the famous **Carnegie Hall** was saved from demolition in New York City.

In 1964, as part of his support for other musicians and artists, he helped create the **National Endowment for the Arts (NEA)**, which still exists today. A highly decorated, much-loved, and unbelievably skilled musician, Isaac Stern spent his entire life pursuing his passion and helping to make sure that others could pursue theirs.

ELISABETH KÜBLER-ROSS was a brilliant **researcher**, **scientist**, and **psychiatrist** who helped deepen the world's understanding of the human mind. Her work on grief and patient care have helped innumerable people around the world cope with traumatic events.

Born on July 8, 1926, in Zürich, Switzerland, Elisabeth's father was a strict, severe man who disapproved of her ambitions. Even as a young girl, Elisabeth expressed a strong desire to study and practice medicine. Her father refused, ordering her instead to either become a maid or to work as a secretary in his business. Neither of these options satisfied Elisabeth, who chose a third option.

In 1942, at only sixteen years of age, Elisabeth left home and began supporting herself. Eventually, after a string of odd jobs, she began serving as a volunteer in war hospitals during World War II. Even after the war had ended, Elisabeth traveled with relief groups to communities that had been damaged by the effects of war. There, she treated refugees and helped in whatever way she could. These experiences only strengthened Elisabeth's desire to work in medicine.

In 1951, Elisabeth took the first step to realize her dream when she enrolled at the University of Zurich. There, she studied medicine and met her future husband, Emanuel Robert Ross. After Elisabeth graduated, the two immigrated to the United States, and they both worked at the Glen Cove Community Hospital in Long Island. Elisabeth discovered her passion for psychiatry there, and she eventually accepted a position at Manhattan State Hospital in the early 1960s.

After almost a decade on the East Coast, Elisabeth and her husband moved to Denver, Colorado, to teach medicine. In Colorado, Elisabeth began her research into the psychology of grief, especially grief concerning death. Elisabeth's research naturally grew into something more than an experiment, and soon her exploration of grief gained national attention from other psychiatrists. So intense was her passion for her research that she eventually stopped teaching entirely to focus on it.

Eventually, Elisabeth developed what she called the "five stages of grief." These five stages were: denial, anger, bargaining, depression, and acceptance. Though Elisabeth first postulated her theory in the late 1960s, these five stages of grief are still used by medical professionals today to help patients deal with loss.

By the time of her own death in 2004, Elisabeth's reputation as one of the twentieth century's finest psychiatrists was undeniable, and she was honored many times by the medical community for her work.

An outstanding **writer**, **educator**, **activist**, and Nobel Prize recipient, **ELIE WIESEL** was a man who dedicated his life to the fight for justice and equality all around the world.

Born on September 30, 1928, in Sighet, Romania, Elie's early life was indelibly marked by tragedy and hardship. As a young man, Elie and his family, along with many other Jewish people from nearby villages, were rounded up by Nazi forces and sent to concentration camps. In those camps, Elie lost both of his parents and his younger sister. Elie survived, however, and in 1945, he and his two older sisters were rescued from the camps by Allied troops.

Following the liberation, Wiesel was taken to safety in Paris, France, in 1948. He resumed his education at the Sorbonne, Europe's second oldest university. While in school, Wiesel also worked as a photojournalist, a career that suited his natural talent for storytelling. By 1956, after encouragement from a friend and fellow student, Wiesel wrote a Yiddish-language memoir titled *Un di velt hot geshvign (And the World Would Remain Silent)*, which told the story of his time in Auschwitz and Buchenwald concentration camps. Later, in 1960, the book was translated into English and French and republished with a new title: *La Nuit*, or *Night*.

Elie Wiesel's memoir was an instant success and captivated thousands of readers around the world who were looking to understand the horrors of the Holocaust. *Night* also made Wiesel a well-known figure in the writing community. When he wrote two more books in the following years titled *Dawn* and *Day*, they, too, were very well-received.

In 1955, Wiesel immigrated to the United States. He met a fellow Holocaust survivor named Marion Rose in America, and they were married. The couple made a new home in New York. For the rest of Wiesel's life, he continued to write, using his success to help speak out against all injustice. As a fierce and passionate advocate, Wiesel was active in almost all major humanitarian conflicts in the mid- to late twentieth century around the world, including South Africa, Rwanda, and Cambodia.

In recognition of his lifetime of good work, Wiesel was honored countless times by governments and organizations around the world. Perhaps the greatest of these came in 1986, when Wiesel was awarded the Nobel Prize for Peace.

Perhaps more than any other figure in modern history, Elie Wiesel was a champion of peace, justice, and equality. He is a fine example of what it means to be a truly good person.

CLAES THURE OLDENBURG is a Swedish American **Pop art sculptor** whose works have shaped contemporary art in America and across the world.

Born on January 28, 1929, in Stockholm, Sweden, Oldenburg's family was both worldly and well-traveled. His father, a diplomat, moved the family between Norway and the United States before officially immigrating to Chicago, Illinois, in 1936. An intelligent, curious child, Oldenburg excelled in the arts and at school in general from a very young age.

As a young man, Oldenburg began studying art history and literature at Yale University. While he initially showed an interest in pursuing a career as a writer, Oldenburg eventually felt himself drawn to physical art. Starting in 1950, he studied at the Art Institute of Chicago, during which time he exercised his strong writing skills in his job as a small-time reporter at the City News Bureau.

In 1956, three years after he officially became a U.S. citizen, Oldenburg moved to New York to continue his career in the arts. He met many prominent artists of his generation, and soon he began to build his own career. During the 1950s and 1960s, Oldenburg became an increasingly common participant in gallery exhibits around the city. These showcased his strange, distorted images of human beings and everyday life.

By 1961, Oldenburg began to focus more on sculpture. He used plaster and other common materials to re-create common objects. His commentary on American culture inducted him into the growing Pop art movement. Oldenburg happily accepted this label, and his works in the 1960s grew larger and more ambitious. Some of these, such as *Placid Civic Monument*, involved a constant cast of performers who acted out a "grave-digging" behind the Metropolitan Museum of Art, New York.

Starting in the 1970s, his works became even larger. These pieces, such as the one at Yale University, were created with the help of his wife Coosje, whom he married in 1977. His most modern works even included a massive, semi-functional boat in the shape of a Swiss Army knife. With a truly unique mind and perspective, Oldenburg constantly pushed the boundaries of what art could be. To date, he has been honored with countless awards recognizing his contributions to modern art.

An enormously talented **author** and fearless **human rights activist**, **CHINUA ACHEBE** was a man who dedicated his life to educating, supporting, and improving life for the Nigerian people and others around the world.

Born on November 16, 1930, as Albert Chinualumogu Achebe in Ogidi, Nigeria, Chinua lived when his homeland was still colonized by the British. His father, a teacher and religious leader, encouraged Chinua's early education and exposed him to works and stories from around the world. This, combined with the strong storytelling tradition of the Igbo people, inspired a lifelong love of stories and writing in the young Chinua.

As a young man, Achebe attended classes at the University College (now the University of Ibadan), where he studied English. Following his later graduation from the college, Achebe accepted a position teaching there. During his time as a professor of English, Achebe continued writing and storytelling. In 1958, he published his first novel, *Things Fall Apart*, which explored the effect of Christian missionaries on the culture of his homeland. Although it was only his first published work, *Things Fall Apart* was met with overwhelming success and Achebe's fame skyrocketed.

In 1961, Achebe left his teaching position at the university in order to begin a career in radio. He worked at the Nigerian Broadcasting Corporation from 1961 to 1966 as the director of external broadcasting. During this period, he wrote three more novels, each similar to his first in the way they talked about issues with colonialism. These novels succeeded in boosting his reputation in the writing community, and in 1967, Achebe worked with poet Christopher Okigbo to create a new organization. This organization, named the Citadel Press, was meant to help create children's books written specifically for African children.

Throughout the late 1960s, Achebe traveled to the United States, where he held events with other writers to inform the American people about the problems plaguing Nigeria. Later, in the 1970s, Achebe held many academic positions at universities in Massachusetts, Connecticut, and back in Nigeria, and he also worked with prominent Nigerian publishers.

Two decades later, after Achebe was partially paralyzed by a tragic car accident in Nigeria, the author officially immigrated to the United States. He taught classes on literature and Africana studies at Bard College and Brown University. A hard-working and dedicated author, he wrote and published numerous novels, essays, and short stories that explored modern African cultures.

Recipient of an impressive number of awards and honors, Chinua Achebe received more than thirty honorary degrees from universities in America and other countries by the time he died in 2013. Today, he is remembered as one of the most important African authors of modern times.

MIKE NICHOLS, originally named Mikhail Igor Peschkowsky, was a German American **director** who worked on countless important productions in television, film, and live theater.

Born on November 6, 1931, in Berlin, Germany, Nichols's family officially immigrated to the United States in 1938, when he was only seven years old. There, Mike found a new home in America as World War II began in Europe. Although Mike often said that he felt completely alone as a child, he made one of his most important friendships as a young man in Chicago. Elaine May, an American comedian, formed an immediate bond with Nichols, which would last the rest of their lives.

Together, the two began performing in comedy sketches in Chicago. Although comedy performers were very common in the city, Nichols and May stood out from the crowd. The pair worked together until 1962, when Mike's career changed direction. Instead of comedy, he began studying and working to become a theater director. He quickly proved to be a natural and won **Tony Awards** for every one of his first three plays.

Also eager to work in movies, Nichols received an Oscar nomination for his very first film, *Who's Afraid of Virginia Woolf?* Although he did not win, his second movie, *The Graduate*, earned him an Oscar victory and launched the career of the movie's star, Dustin Hoffman.

Throughout his career, Nichols worked on and directed an amazing number of plays and films, many of which are seen today as timeless classics. During his time as a director, Nichols worked with some of the finest young actors before most people knew who they were. Robin Williams, Natalie Portman, Jude Law, and others all starred in Nichols's films when they were only just beginning their acting careers.

Today, modern American film experts argue that Nichols ushered in a new era of American cinema. While his early work, including his comedy, was lighter and more carefree, he slowly shifted to a darker, more serious style. This pattern holds true for other artists of the time, but few as strongly as Nichols.

An overwhelmingly important piece of American cinema history, Nichols helped to shape the industry into what it is today. Throughout his career, he not only created several masterpieces, but also gave many of the biggest actors of the twentieth century their jumpstart in the industry.

◆ A talented Japanese American **musician** and **composer**, SEIJI OZAWA'S unique style and emotional performances have set him apart and made him one of the most popular conductors of the twentieth and twenty-first centuries.

Born on September 1, 1935, in what is now China, Seiji Ozawa began studying music, specifically piano, as a very young child. Although Ozawa was a hugely talented young musician, showing impressive potential as a pianist, his future in performance was cut short when he was sixteen because a tragic accident left him with serious injuries in both hands. Though the injuries meant the end of his piano performance career, Ozawa soon found a new path in conducting.

When he was still in high school in China, he traveled to learn from the legendary Hideo Saito at the Toho School of Music in Japan. From there, Ozawa's skill and knowledge of conducting grew. After working with his mentor, Ozawa went on to conduct for the Japan Broadcasting System and the Japanese Philharmonic Orchestra.

Later, in 1959, Ozawa moved to Europe, where he worked and toured as a professional conductor. He won the International Conductors' Competition, bringing him much respect and recognition from his peers. In the years following, Ozawa continued to learn and perform, visiting and studying with Europe's finest musicians. A lifelong student, Ozawa made it a priority to continue learning throughout his entire career.

In the 1960s, Seiji Ozawa moved to the United States to continue his career. From 1964 to 1976, he served as a music director for many well-respected organizations, such as Chicago's Ravinia Festival, the Toronto Symphony Orchestra, and the San Francisco Orchestra. In 1973, Ozawa took on a job as music director of the famous Boston Symphony Orchestra (BSO), which he kept for almost three decades. Ozawa's time as director of the BSO was the longest of any conductor in American orchestral history.

Although most of his efforts focused on Boston during this time, he also accepted invitations to travel the world and guest conduct for other organizations. Throughout the 1980s and 1990s, Ozawa began creating several musical organizations to support the musical community. Specifically, he founded the Saito Kinen Organization in honor of his first mentor when he was just a teenager.

While health concerns and age have slowed Seiji Ozawa's performances in the twenty-first century, he remains active within the musical world and he strongly supports other conductors and musicians. Many say he is one of the greatest conductors of his time, and his influence on modern classical music cannot be measured.

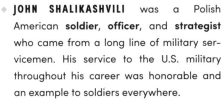

JOHN SHALIKASHVILI was a Polish American **soldier**, **officer**, and **strategist** who came from a long line of military servicemen. His service to the U.S. military throughout his career was honorable and an example to soldiers everywhere.

Born on June 27, 1936, as John Malchase David Shalikashvili in Warsaw, Poland, Shalikashvili lived in Poland until he was sixteen years old. His father was a Polish military officer who fought against German forces in World War II, and his grandfather was a decorated general for the Russian army. In 1952, Shalikashvili immigrated with his family to Peoria, Illinois, and they began their life in America. Although Shalikashvili spoke very little English when he first moved with his family, he worked hard and learned quickly. Interestingly, he said that he learned much of his English through watching John Wayne cowboy movies.

Only a few years later in 1958, Shalikashvili was drafted into the U.S. **Army**. Once enlisted, he applied for Officer Candidate School and was commissioned as a second lieutenant only one year later. Shalikashvili proved to be an excellent soldier, and over the next decade, he was stationed at posts throughout the United States. In 1968, however, he was sent to his first post in Vietnam.

In Vietnam, Shalikashvili worked as an adviser for the South Vietnamese military. After completing his tour of duty, John moved on to different countries across Europe. In 1991, Shalikashvili received an honor and recognition for his efforts in Operation: Provide Comfort when he organized forces from various countries to aid refugees in Iraq.

One year later in 1992, Shalikashvili was promoted to the position of supreme commander of North Atlantic Treaty

Organization (NATO) forces in Europe, a very important and difficult job. When Colin Powell retired from his post as chairman of the Joint Chiefs of Staff in 1993, he personally recommended John Shalikashvili to President Bill Clinton as his replacement. The president agreed, and Shalikashvili was soon confirmed. Importantly, this made John the first foreign-born person to ever hold the position.

Throughout his career, Shalikashvili was known by his colleagues and superiors as a man of impressive work ethic and dedication to his job. A man who "got things done," Shalikashvili was one of America's best, and he helped stabilize and support people around the world. Today, he is remembered as an example of America's finest. His legacy as a great soldier and a good man will inspire service personnel and civilians for years to come.

ANDREW GROVE was a Hungarian American **entrepreneur** and **entrepreneur** who was hugely successful in American business throughout his life. His companies employed thousands of people and helped create some of the most important technology we use today.

Originally born András István Grófon on September 2, 1936, in Budapest, Hungary, to a Jewish family, Grove and his family survived many terrifying and dangerous events in his early life. After living through both Nazi and communist control of his home country, Grove finally decided to leave in 1956. Although he spent a short time in Austria, he quickly immigrated to the United States to begin his new life.

In the United States, Grove settled in New York and began attending courses at the City College. To support himself, he worked hard at a restaurant while attending school full time. In 1960, he earned his bachelor's degree in chemical engineering. Still hungry for more education, Grove moved to California and enrolled in university. In 1963, he received his doctorate in chemical engineering from the University of California, Berkeley.

Wasting no time, Grove quickly found a job as a researcher at the Fairchild Semiconductor Corporation, which was developing cutting-edge technology. Later, when leadership from Fairchild left to start the famous Intel Corporation, Grove was brought along as a key member of the company. At Intel, Grove worked in many different positions, including chief executive office and chair.

In 1971, Intel and Grove made history when they announced the invention of the microprocessor, which helped revolutionize computer technology. Over the next several decades, Intel would invent and manufacture many more improved microchips.

Although many scientists and engineers worked for Intel during this time, historians give much of the credit for the company's success to Andrew Grove. Specifically, Grove had a reputation as a fair, capable manager who encouraged employees to ask questions and solve problems together. His presence at Intel made sure that everything ran smoothly. Although he was highly paid and widely respected, Grove worked from a simple, plain cubicle at the company just like any other employee.

Later, in 1977, Andrew Grove was named *TIME* magazine's Man of the Year. Although he passed away in 2016, Andrew is remembered today as one of the most important businessmen of the twentieth and twenty-first centuries. He was a brilliant, dedicated, and humble man who made everyone around him better. Without him, we would not have much of the technology we use every day.

Egyptian American **scientist**, **space geologist**, and **researcher FAROUK EL-BAZ** helped advance humanity's understanding of the universe for more than half a century.

Born on January 2, 1938, in Al-Zaqāzīq, Egypt, El-Baz spent his entire childhood and much of his early adult life in his homeland of Egypt. By the age of twenty, he had earned bachelor's degrees in chemistry and geology from Ain Shams University. Following his graduation, however, he immigrated to the United States to pursue opportunities in higher education.

In 1961, El-Baz received his master's degree in geology from the Missouri School of Mines and Metallurgy (present-day Missouri University of Science and Technology). Three years later, after performing research at MIT, he earned his doctoral degree from the same school. Although still quite young, Farouk quickly became one of the top experts in geology, and his reputation among colleagues continued to grow.

After a short period teaching as a professor of geology at different universities, El-Baz was invited to help National Aeronautics and Space Administration (NASA). There, he worked as supervisor of the Lunar Science Planning program to prepare astronauts and the team for the **Apollo 11** mission. In addition to his supervisory duties, El-Baz was also tasked with other key parts of the mission. He worked directly with scientists of all types and the astronauts themselves. After the mission was completed, El-Baz left NASA to work with other organizations and companies.

For almost a decade starting in 1972, El-Baz created and managed the Center for Earth and Planetary Studies, which observed the Earth and took advanced photographs for researchers.

By 1978, after El-Baz had returned to his home country to work, he was chosen by

President Anwar Sadat to serve as the country's science adviser. El-Baz was so skilled at this job that, after only a few years, he was awarded Egypt's Order of Merit—First Class by the president.

Throughout his career, Farouk El-Baz has received countless other awards, merits, and honors for his extremely impressive work and service. A valuable member to many governments and organizations, Farouk has helped scientists around the world in their research and programs. Although he began his work more than sixty years ago, he continues to discover new ways to use technology to benefit humankind. Specifically, El-Baz developed a way to use images taken from space to detect water in deserts around the world.

El-Baz continues his work today as an adviser for the Egyptian government, demonstrating yet again his dedication and tireless work ethic.

◆ An **author** and **human rights activist**, **BETTE BAO LORD** works to make the world a better, more understanding place for people everywhere. In particular, her novels help Americans better understand the Chinese culture.

Born on November 3, 1938, in Shanghai, China, Bette immigrated to the United States with her family when she was eight years old. Her father, who had been trained in engineering by the British, was ordered to travel to the United States to procure equipment for the Chinese government. When communist leader Mao Zedong won the Chinese civil war in 1949, however, Bette and her family were unable to return to their home country. Instead, they settled near Brooklyn, New York, and started a new life.

As a young girl, Bette attended public school in New York and became a dedicated student. After secondary school, she continued her education, earning a bachelor's degree in political science from Tufts University and, later, a master's degree from the Fletcher School of Law and Diplomacy. In 1962, she married Winston Lord, a foreign service officer, who later went on to serve as the U.S. ambassador to China.

A bright and ambitious young woman, Lord quickly went to work after finishing her schooling. Even at the beginning of her career, Lord knew that she wanted to do something to make the world a better place. In 1962, her sister, who had been trapped in China, finally escaped with the help of her mother and joined her family in the United States. These events inspired Lord to write her first book, *Eighth Moon: The True Story of a Young Girl's Life in Communist China.*

Lord's writing skill and the relatable, emotional story inspired by her own life and her sister's escape made the book an instant success. She was encouraged by the strength of her first novel and continued writing. In 1981, she published perhaps her most famous book, *Spring Moon: A Novel of China*, which was about a rich, young Chinese girl in the early 1900s. For this work, Bette Bao Lord received an American Book Award nomination. In recognition of her career and life story, she was awarded the first ever Eleanor Roosevelt Award for Human Rights by President Bill Clinton in 1998.

Not satisfied with only writing, Lord used her newfound success to advocate for justice. With her eloquence and charismatic personality, she still champions worthy causes around the world today. Throughout modern American history, there have been few women as graceful, brave, and talented as Bette Bao Lord.

◆ **KWAME TURE**, born as Stokely Carmichael, was a prominent **civil rights activist** and leader who fought against racism and discrimination in mid-twentieth-century America. He took his new name as an adult in order to honor two African leaders.

Born on June 29, 1941, in Trinidad and Tobago, Ture immigrated to New York City with his family when he was only eleven years old. He attended public school in a largely Italian and Jewish neighborhood of the Bronx. Both of Ture's parents were hard workers, and they passed down that work ethic to their son, who excelled in school. After high school, in 1960, Ture began attending classes at Howard University.

Ture became an active member of many student activist groups such as the Student Nonviolent Coordinating Committee (SNCC) and the Freedom Riders movement. These organizations aimed to peacefully protest racist rules and laws throughout the country. This type of protest was known as civil disobedience, and was popular in the era of Martin Luther King Jr. In one instance, when Ture participated in a Freedom Ride on the public bus system, he was arrested by police and jailed for almost two months.

This experience only strengthened Ture's determination to protest, but the treatment of his peaceful friends and fellow activists began to anger him. In 1966, during a SNCC march in Mississippi, Ture gave a speech that would inspire the formation of the Black Power movement. Unlike other groups, the Black Power movement argued that African Americans should learn self-defense. Additionally, Ture and his partners emphasized the need for increased Black financial and political power. Radically different from the philosophy of Martin Luther King Jr., who advocated for peace and diplomacy, the Black Power movement frightened many white Americans.

In the late 1960s, Ture began traveling across the country and internationally to protest racial discrimination in the United States. During this time, he met with many activist leaders and became a vocal pro-tester of the Vietnam War. In 1969, frustrated with the politics of the United States, Ture and his wife moved to West Africa, where he helped create the All-African People's Revolutionary Party (A-APRP).

For the rest of his life, Ture would occasionally return to the United States to visit friends or speak at events. Despite this, his philosophy had changed. Ture believed that the only way for Black citizens of the world to truly be free was to build a strong and united Africa. Today, he is remembered as a fierce champion of justice who refused to compromise his beliefs.

A world-renowned **journalist** and best-selling **author, ISABEL ALLENDE** is a Chilean American woman of great personal drive and grace. She came from humble beginnings and rose to become one of the most respected female authors of the twentieth century.

Born on August 2, 1942, in Lima, Peru, her childhood was marked with personal challenges and hardship. Though Isabel was the goddaughter of Salvador Allende, Chile's first socialist president, she and her mother struggled financially. This was because Isabel's father, a politician, had deserted them when she was very young. After Isabel's mother remarried another politician, the family moved often and suddenly.

Partly because of this, Allende began pursuing a career as a journalist when she was a young woman. She showed a strong natural talent for the profession, and by the 1960s and 1970s, she started working for television companies and magazines in South America.

In 1973, however, Chile was thrown into chaos when General Augusto Pinochet violently overthrew the government in a military junta, killing Isabel's godfather in the process. Spurred into action, Allende worked to protect Pinochet's many victims. By 1975, however, Chile had become an incredibly dangerous place to live, and Allende was forced to flee the country with her family. Together, they lived in Venezuela for thirteen years, unable to return home.

Throughout the 1980s, Allende began to explore writing. She wrote her first novel, *The House of Spirits*, which was published in 1985. The book was an immediate success, and Isabel Allende quickly became a respected and world-renowned author. Encouraged by her first book's success, she continued to write. She produced more than a dozen novels between the late 1980s and 2015, many of which also became best-sellers. Like many popular South American authors of her generation, Allende wrote in a style known as **magical realism**, in which she portrayed the modern world with added magical elements. In 1987, Allende moved to San Francisco, California, to continue her work, and in 1993, she officially became a U.S. citizen.

Over the course of her career, Isabel Allende has received many awards and honors for her work, including one Chilean national prize for literature. In 2014, Isabel was even awarded the Presidential Medal of Freedom by President Barack Obama, who was a fan.

Although she suffered throughout her life, Allende turned her suffering into beauty through writing, persevering through tragedy and hardship to build a better life for herself. For many artists and authors around the world, she is a shining example of the power of storytelling.

◆ **DITH PRAN** was a Cambodian American **activist** and **photojournalist** whose vivid and brave photos exposed the horrors of the Khmer Rouge to international audiences.

Born on September 27, 1942, in Siem Reap, Cambodia, Pran lived much of his early life under foreign control. When he was a young child, Cambodia was occupied by Japanese forces but legally was territory of French Indochina. Despite this, Pran's childhood was relatively peaceful. He lived in a rural area of Cambodia with his family, near the world-famous temple Angkor Wat.

After World War II, however, that peaceful life began to fade. In the east of Pran's home in Vietnam, French soldiers fought against communist forces. Even after the communist Vietnamese forced the French soldiers to leave, the fighting did not stop. Because of this, soldiers from both North and South Vietnam would often cross into Cambodia to hide. During the Vietnam War, American forces began to enter Cambodia illegally, too. Cambodia subsequently broke off its agreements with the United States in 1965 and demanded that they leave the country.

Following these events, Dith Pran began working with British filmmakers in his country as a guide and interpreter. This would become a common job for Pran, who was both brave and intelligent enough to keep them safe. In 1975, after a violent group known as the Khmer Rouge took control, many Cambodians tried to flee. During this time, Pran worked with other reporters to cover the events. At one point, Pran saved the lives of foreign journalists by convincing soldiers to let them go free.

Despite his heroism, Dith Pran was left behind when his foreign journalist friends fled. He was trapped in the Khmer Rouge-controlled country and barely survived. In 1979, after the Khmer Rouge was finally overthrown, Pran was finally able to travel to the United States and reunite with his family. In the United States, he became a reporter for the *New York Times*.

Although his new life with his family in the United States was much safer, Pran never forgot his homeland. Over the next several years, he visited Cambodia often to help those who had also suffered. Additionally, Pran and his wife created the Dith Pran Holocaust Awareness Project. This organization used photojournalism to document the crimes of the Khmer Rouge, in hopes that they might one day be brought to justice.

Although Dith Pran passed away in 2008, he remains a symbol of outstanding bravery and dedication to justice. His legacy is an example of true courage.

◆ **MARIO MOLINA**, a Mexican American **scientist** and Nobel Prize-winning **chemist**, made discoveries that helped humankind understand the growing dangers of climate change. His work provided the world with a somber warning to treat our planet better, before it is too late.

Born on March 19, 1943, in Mexico City, Mexico, Mario José Molina was fascinated by the sciences for as long as he could remember. As a child attending primary school in the city, he would play for hours in his homemade laboratory with crude, basic instruments. This passion stayed with him for his entire life. His aunt, Esther, was also a chemist. She challenged and encouraged him to pursue his dreams, but not even she could have predicted what Molina would become.

At eleven years of age, Molina was sent overseas to a boarding school in Switzerland. He studied German and other subjects, but his focus was always on chemistry. Although he briefly considered a career playing the violin, he stayed true to his dream. In 1960, Molina began attending classes on chemical engineering at the National Autonomous University of Mexico. After he graduated with his bachelor's degree, Molina began searching for other opportunities in higher education. His search took him to Germany, where he spent two years at the University of Freiburg. Still unsatisfied, however, he decided to spend some time in Paris where he studied politics, art, and philosophy.

In 1968, at twenty-five years old, Molina emigrated from his home in Mexico to the United States. He began a graduate program at the University of California, Berkeley. Finally, he could truly study his passion: chemistry. At Berkeley, Molina's skill grew amazingly fast. By 1972 he had completed his doctoral degree, but he stayed at the school for another year to continue his research.

After leaving Berkeley, Molina went on to work with Professor Sherry Rowland, who gave him a choice of research topic. Mario chose to study the chemistry of Earth's atmosphere. Three months later, Molina and Rowland developed a theory about ozone depletion. Together, the pair discovered that harmful chemicals known as CFCs, or chlorofluorocarbons, were slowly destroying the Earth's ozone layer. They worked even harder on their research.

In 1974, when they published the results of their study, they had hoped that other scientists and politicians would see their work and take action. They knew that the Earth needed our help—and fast. For his research, Molina was awarded the Nobel Prize for Chemistry.

Today, the work of Mario Molina is the foundation of many efforts to help protect our planet. Because of his curiosity, brilliance, and dedication to the sciences, humankind is now working to help fix climate change—and save our planet.

ITZHAK PERLMAN is renowned as a genius **musician** whose performances on the violin have stunned audiences around the world and established him as one of the greatest violinists of his time.

Born on August 31, 1945, in Israel, Perlman loved music from a very young age. By the age of three, Itzhak had already begun practicing on the violin. At age four, however, he fell sick with polio. Although the disease affected his legs, it could not dampen his passion, and after he recovered, he continued his musical education. To encourage his growth, his parents enrolled him at the Tel Aviv Academy of Music. In 1955, when Itzhak was only ten years old, he gave his first official violin concert.

In 1958, Perlman was sent to the United States to continue learning. There, he was enrolled at the Juilliard School in New York where he studied under some of the finest music teachers of the twentieth century. Always loving to perform, thirteen-year-old Perlman played the violin for a national television audience on the *Ed Sullivan Show*. The young man's appearance was a huge success, and in the following years, he continued to perform on large stages.

In 1963, Perlman played at the famous Carnegie Hall, and his performance was so impressive that he received the Leventritt Prize. A rare and precious honor, the prize helped Perlman's reputation in the music world skyrocket. Soon, he began to play with the best American orchestras around the country. Perlman also performed with jazz groups and played with traditional Jewish musicians whenever he could.

During his career, Itzhak Perlman was invited to play for film music, including the Oscar-winning score of *Schindler's List*.

Later in life, Perlman began to work more as a conductor. From 2001 to 2005, he conducted for the respected Detroit Symphony while also working as an adviser for the St. Louis Symphony. He taught classes, gave lectures, and even created organizations with his wife to help support young musicians.

Throughout his career, Perlman won an amazing fifteen Grammys. He also received the National Medal of Arts and the Presidential Medal of Freedom among other significant accolades. Now in his later years, Itzhak Perlman has dedicated much of his time to helping promote music and the arts.

A genius and master of his craft, Perlman is an inspiration for musicians all over the world.

A man who has worn many hats in his life, **ARNOLD SCHWARZENEGGER** has been a champion **bodybuilder**, blockbuster **movie star**, and even a U.S. **governor**. This Austrian American powerhouse is larger than life and has always tried to use his influence to improve the world.

Born on July 30, 1947, in Graz, Austria, Arnold's childhood was marked by personal and family struggles. His father was a member of the Nazi Party during World War II, and the experience left him a depressed and troubled man. Although Arnold knew early on that he wanted to be a bodybuilder, his father often mocked his dreams. Because of this treatment, Arnold developed a strong love for movies. As a boy, he would watch films starring bodybuilders and action stars, dreaming of his future.

These films also encouraged Schwarzenegger's fascination with America. In order to get to the United States, he worked hard on his bodybuilding and eventually met Joe Weider, who ran the International Federation of Bodybuilding and Fitness. Joe saw huge potential in Schwarzenegger right away and helped the young man move to the United States. Joe was right, and during his career as a bodybuilder, Schwarzenegger won eleven bodybuilding titles.

Many believe that it was Schwarzenegger's good looks and charming personality that encouraged bodybuilding's popularity in the 1970s and beyond. Always ambitious, however, Schwarzenegger began to seek out acting jobs. Because of his body and strength, studios knew right away that Schwarzenegger would make a world-class action star. In the 1980s, Arnold starred in Hollywood blockbuster films like *Conan the Barbarian* and the *Terminator* franchise. These roles helped Schwarzenegger's reputation grow until eventually he was a world-famous actor.

In 2003, Schwarzenegger's ambition reared its head again when he joined the race for governor of California. Although many didn't believe that a former bodybuilder and movie star could win, Schwarzenegger proved them wrong. As governor, Schwarzenegger worked hard to improve life for Californians. He focused on the economy for his two terms. After leaving public office, Schwarzenegger returned to making movies. Still a world-famous star, he continued making more successful movies.

Arnold Schwarzenegger's determination, ambition, and work ethic has inspired so many. He is one of the most beloved and recognizable figures of the twentieth and early twenty-first centuries.

DEEPAK CHOPRA, an Indian American **author, public speaker**, and **healer**, became known around the world for his deep understanding of mental and physical health. Over his lifetime, he has helped many to live better lives.

Born on October 22, 1947, in New Delhi, India, Chopra's childhood goals were strongly influenced by his father, a famous cardiologist. While Chopra wanted to study journalism and not medicine at first, he soon changed his mind. Chopra saw just how important medicine could be for humanity.

As a young man, Chopra began attending classes at the All India Institute of Medical Sciences in New Delhi. There, he focused almost entirely on traditional Western medicine. Like his father, Chopra was fascinated by modern technology and techniques. In 1970, after he graduated, Chopra immigrated to the United States with almost nothing to his name. There, he began his medical residency in at Muhlenberg Hospital in Plainfield, New Jersey, where he lived.

After his residency, Chopra moved to Boston. There, his skill set and responsibilities grew until he became the chief of medicine at New England Memorial Hospital. Although Chopra was very talented and highly respected as a doctor of Western medicine, he soon grew frustrated with his work. While he was very good at treating physical illnesses, Chopra felt that modern medicine was both unhappy and unhealthy for the mind and spirit.

These feelings grew, and soon Chopra began exploring alternative medicine. Working with a famous guru named Maharishi Mahesh Yogi, Deepak developed a new type of medical practice focusing on wellness and holistic, or complete, health. He quit his job as chief of medicine in Boston to focus on his new path.

As Deepak Chopra's ideas began to spread, he gained the attention of many American celebrities. In the 1980s, he continued to improve his treatments until 1995, when he opened The Chopra Center. Patients from around the world flock there to find health and inner peace. The success of Chopra's practice grew more when he began writing books. By the time his second book, *Ageless Body, Timeless Mind*, was published in 1993, Chopra had become a household name. Today, many believe in self-care, but few know that these ideas came from people like Deepak Chopra.

Although controversial at times, Chopra has always been dedicated to improving the lives of his patients. His alternative medicine, focused on treating the entire person, has helped many find new meaning and balance in their lives.

A Russian American **dancer** and **choreographer**, **MIKHAIL BARYSHNIKOV'S** work has stunned audiences for more than fifty years. As one of the greatest ballet dancers of his time, Baryshnikov's influence on modern ballet is undeniable.

Born on January 27, 1948, in Riga, Latvia, Mikhail struggled in his family life as a young man. His father was a colonel in the Soviet military, and he disapproved of Mikhail's ballet ambitions. To make things worse, Mikhail's mother passed away tragically when he was only sixteen years old. At about the same time, Mikhail began to study the art of ballet.

He was a natural at dance, and soon he was training under the well-respected Alexander Pushkin at the Vaganova ballet school (present-day Mariinsky Theatre ballet school) in St. Petersburg. In 1967, only three years after Baryshnikov began training, he performed for the first time on stage with the Kirov Ballet in *Giselle*. The performance was an enormous success, and his reputation as a young ballet prodigy was established. From there, Baryshnikov continued to grow more adept and famous.

In 1966, the young dancer won a gold medal at the Varna International Ballet Competition in Bulgaria. Three years later, in 1969, he won another gold at the Moscow International Ballet Competition. Not only was Baryshnikov a technically perfect ballet dancer, he was also able to pour emotion into every one of his performances. By the 1970s, Mikhail Baryshnikov was considered one of the finest dancers in all of Soviet Russia.

For Baryshnikov, however, the political unrest of his home country was both frustrating and distracting. Because of this, he left Soviet Russia and fled to Canada in 1974. Once in Canada, he quickly immigrated to the United States, where he joined the world-famous American Ballet Theatre (ABT). Again, Baryshnikov grew to be one of the most impressive ballet dancers in the country. So great was his popularity that he even acted in movies and danced on television during the 1970s and 1980s.

In 1980, Baryshnikov took a position as the artistic director of the ABT. There, he used his natural talent and experience to help teach and guide other dancers. Later on in his career, he began to create his own ballet and art organizations, and he remained active in theater productions.

To date, Mikhael Baryshnikov has not once sacrificed his beliefs. He followed his dreams and worked hard to make them reality. He has inspired a legion of artists in America and around the world through his artistry.

◆ **GRACE JONES**, a Jamaican American **model**, **actress**, and **musician** became known for her striking appearance and bold personality, making her one of the most recognizable faces of her time.

Born on May 19, 1948, in Spanish Town, Jamaica, Grace was raised for most of her childhood by her grandparents. This was because her father, who was a politician, worked in the United States. As a young girl, Grace discovered a natural talent for sports. As she continued to grow, Grace became a tall, strong woman with a unique look that made her perfect for modeling.

At thirteen years old, Jones moved to New York to finish her schooling. After graduating, she enrolled at Onondaga Community College (OCC) where she began studying Spanish. Jones, however, was fascinated by theater. She dropped out of college to work on plays with a drama professor, who she followed to Philadelphia. There, her love for theater and performance grew, and she knew that she had made the right decision.

When Jones was eighteen, she was signed by the Wilhelmina Models talent management agency, which scouted her for her striking features. Although she had been bullied as a child for her appearance, Jones was able to use her appearance to quickly become one of the most recognizable models in the United States. She worked with famous brands in both high fashion and makeup during her career.

Jones was not satisfied with only modeling, however, and as a young woman, she began a musical career. In 1977 she released her debut album, titled *Portfolio*. It was a success, and Grace was encouraged to continue releasing albums throughout the 1970s and 1980s.

In 1985, Jones's career expanded once more when she appeared in the James

Bond film *A View to a Kill*. The movie was very popular, and Jones earned a reputation as a skilled and serious actress. Over the course of her career, Jones would star in many more blockbuster Hollywood movies such as *Conan the Destroyer* with Arnold Schwarzenegger (see no. 82).

A multitalented woman who excelled in many different careers during her life, Grace Jones has never let other people decide her future for her. She discovered her passions early in life and never stopped working to make them a reality. A woman of incredible beauty, ambition, intelligence, and skill, Jones inspires artists everywhere and is an example of what hard work and determination can bring.

Through persistence and determination, **author, entrepreneur**, and **activist ARIANNA HUFFINGTON** made herself one of the most successful women of her time.

Born Arianna Stassinopoulos on July 15, 1950, in Athens, Arianna spent her early childhood in Greece. But when she was still a teenager, she moved to England so that she could enroll at the University of Cambridge, where she studied economics. Also at Cambridge, Arianna joined the university's debate club and was the first non-English student to serve as its president. For the rest of her life, Arianna's knowledge of economics and debate would help her become a successful entrepreneur.

After graduating, she lived and worked in London for many years. In 1974, she published her first novel, *The Female Woman*. In 1980, the same year that she immigrated to the United States, she published her second novel, *After Reason*.

In the United States, she settled in California and continued her writing career. During 1986, she married her husband, Michael Huffington, a Republican politician, and they started a family.

Although Arianna Huffington was originally very politically conservative, her views changed over time. Specifically, she began to support "green" initiatives, and she believed in reforming the way that big companies worked within the United States in order to prevent corruption.

In 2005, Huffington created her most famous business venture, *The Huffington Post*. At first, it was only a small online blog that covered mostly liberal ideas, but *The Huffington Post* slowly grew in the years after it was created. Today, the website is considered one of the largest and most influential news blogs in the world, and many thousands visit it each day. In a smart

business move, Huffington sold the website to the AOL company for $300 million in 2011.

Even while running her business, Huffington still found time to continue her writing career. She wrote and published several best-selling books on different topics, including biographies of famous musicians and some business titles. She was also included on *TIME* magazine's 100 Most Powerful Women list multiple years in a row.

In addition to her other work, Huffington also created Thrive Global, a health-and-wellness venture, continuing to push herself and the people around her to be better. An inspiration to people everywhere, Huffington serves as a high-level example of how hard work can pay off.

Egyptian American **professor** and **scientist WAFAA EL-SADR** has greatly improved humanity's understanding of health and diseases. Her research has saved the lives of countless around the world.

Born in 1950 in Egypt, El-Sadr's family was full of doctors and scientists. Her brother was a doctor, her mother was a forensic pathologist, and her father was a biochemist. Because of this, she knew from an early age that she wanted to study science and medicine. Her family supported her and helped her become an extremely smart and skilled scientist.

As a young woman, El-Sadr enrolled at Cairo University in Egypt. This was the same school where both of her parents had taught and worked. Her time there was very different from her time at schools in the United States and Europe. Because many Egyptian schools did not have the advanced technology of Western institutions, much of the training focused on how to talk to patients and use their reported symptoms to diagnose an illness.

After she completed her schooling in Cairo, where she focused on parasitic infections, Wafaa El-Sadr immigrated to the United States in 1976. Although she originally only wanted to live in the United States temporarily, she soon changed her mind and made it her new home. El-Sadr's timing was very fortunate for America, as in the 1970s and 1980s, HIV—or, human immunodeficiency virus—was rampant. As one of the most brilliant and creative medical minds of her generation, El-Sadr was well equipped to help battle the disease.

Soon after she arrived in the United States, El-Sadr worked her way up to chief of the infectious diseases division of Harlem Hospital in New York. In those years, Harlem was hit especially hard by the HIV/AIDS epidemic, and El-Sadr worked every day to help citizens of the city. While there, she helped create amazing methods and technology to treat and respond to the disease, saving thousands.

Wafaa El-Sadr's reputation grew both in her community and around the world. She quickly became one of the world's top experts in HIV/AIDS and worked with other scientists to keep improving treatments for the disease.

After establishing herself in the fight against HIV/AIDS, Wafaa El-Sadr continued working, teaching, and researching new ways to treat a number of diseases, spending much of her time in Africa treating patients in areas with very few doctors. Her brilliant mind, brave spirit, and kind heart make her one of the most impressive people of the last century.

Although many people have worked hard to improve computer technology in the twentieth and twenty-first centuries, very few have been as important or influential as **BJARNE STROUSTRUP**. A Danish American **computer programmer** and professor, Stroustrup helped create **C++,** a very popular programming language.

Born on December 30, 1950, in Aarhus, Denmark, Bjarne enjoyed a very normal childhood. The son of middle-class parents, Bjarne worked hard in school and knew early on that he wanted to study mathematics and computers.

In 1969, Stroustrup enrolled at Aarhus University in his hometown. There, he attended classes on computer science with a focus on microprogramming and machine architecture. In 1975, Stroustrup graduated with a master's degree from the same university. Four years later, he graduated again from the University of Cambridge, where he earned a doctoral degree in computer science. After leaving Cambridge, Stroustrup immigrated to the United States to live and work.

Immediately after finishing his education, Stroustrup was hired by Bell Labs to join the Computer Science Research Center in Murray Hill, New Jersey. There, he worked with other like-minded computer experts to create new, advanced technologies. His most noted invention, though, was a computer language known as C++. With this language, computer manufacturers and software designers could build new, state-of-the-art programs.

Unlike other computer languages, which were mostly used for specific tasks, C++ could be used for almost anything. Whether a programmer was working on a video game, banking application, or airplane systems, C++ was perfect. Even today, decades later, C++ is still learned and used by almost all computer programmers.

Since developing his language, Stroustrup has continued to work and improve computer technology. He has written many books and papers on the subject, and he also guest lectures at colleges around the country. Together with other computer scientists of his generation, Stroustrup has invented some of the most important devices and technologies of the modern era.

Stroustrup is also a very skilled entrepreneur, and has spent time working as a managing director for Morgan Stanley, one of America's most respected investment firms, in New York City. He has also taught at Columbia University and Texas A&M University, helping the next generation learn about computers.

Of all the modern-day comforts and inventions, very few are as important as the computer. Bjarne Stroustrup helped to improve these machines, making them more useful, reliable, and flexible. His work has inspired thousands of students and inventors, and his language C++ is now known by across the world.

An Algerian American **scientist, radiologist,** and **inventor** who has helped save countless lives, **ELIAS ZERHOUNI** is known as a man of impressive dedication and intelligence, whose work has made the world a better place.

Born on April 1, 1951, in the tiny village of Nedroma, Algeria, Zerhouni's family was full of very intelligent people. In 1953, when Elias was only two years old, his family moved from their village to Algiers, the country's capital city. His father, a professor of mathematics, encouraged Zerhouni to do well in school from a young age. As a young man, Zerhouni attended the University of Algiers School of Medicine, where he received excellent grades.

After he graduated, Elias Zerhouni was inspired to study radiology, which used radio-wave–based technology to help diagnose and treat patients. This decision was in part influenced by Zerhouni's uncle, who was also a brilliant and well-respected radiologist. After Zerhouni earned his medical degree at twenty-four years old, the young doctor immigrated to the United States to continue learning and work.

In the United States, Zerhouni quickly found a new home. Although he could only speak very limited English, he was eventually hired by Johns Hopkins University School of Medicine. There, he worked as a radiology resident. In only three years at Johns Hopkins, Zerhouni eventually became chief resident, and in the late 1970s, he also joined the university faculty there. During his time at Johns Hopkins, Zerhouni researched and developed a method to identify whether or not spots in a patient's lungs were malignant, or cancerous. This method is still used today to predict disease and save lives.

In 1981, Zerhouni left Johns Hopkins to continue his career. He was hired as vice-chair of radiology at Eastern Virginia Medical School, where he researched and discovered even more ways to use radiology to detect diseases. This became a trend for him. Throughout his career, Zerhouni continued to improve technology in creative and brilliant ways. More than anything, Elias always looked for a way to improve life for his patients.

By 2002, Elias Zerhouni had become one of the most respected medical professionals in the United States. Because of this, he was asked by President George W. Bush to serve as director of the National Institute of Health (NIH). Zerhouni accepted, and as director, he helped transform the institute. Focusing on new research techniques, Zerhouni advanced American medical science at an unbelievable rate.

Perhaps more than any other medical scientist, Elias Zerhouni has catapulted modern medicine into what it is today. His work and discoveries have helped save countless lives, and he is an inspiration to scientists everywhere.

◆ **DAVID HO**, a Taiwanese American **scientist, researcher**, and **doctor**, has helped expand our understanding of many different viruses, including AIDS, or acquired immunodeficiency syndrome. His work has saved more lives than could ever be counted.

Born on November 3, 1952, in Taichung, Taiwan, David Ho was the son of poor but hard-working parents. His father was an engineer who believed in his son and encouraged him to dream big. In order to provide a better life for his family, David's father, Paul, left home for America, where he worked hard. While he was away, David's mother was also very supportive of her son, and as a child, David excelled in school. Specifically, David discovered a passion for math and science at a very early age.

By 1965, David's father had successfully made a good home, and so David and his family emigrated from Taiwan to America to be with him. In their new home in Los Angeles, California, David continued his schooling. Although David spoke no English when he first arrived in America, he learned quickly and continued to excel in math. After only six months in the United States, David had become fluent in English.

After high school, Ho began classes at MIT on the East Coast. After a short while, in 1974, he became homesick for California and transferred to the California Institute of Technology (Caltech). He discovered molecular biology at Caltech and quickly made it his focus. Thanks to this, he went on to earn a medical degree from Harvard University.

As a young professional, Ho immediately began making many discoveries about viruses. He was only the fourth scientist in the world to identify HIV. For the rest of his career, Ho was one of the most important people in the world when it came to fighting HIV. After he isolated the virus, Ho continued his research, looking for ways to fight it. While working on the science of the virus, he also helped calm the public, who were very frightened.

Other scientists helped Ho with his research, and all of them worked together to defeat the terrible virus. Although there is still no cure for HIV today, the work of Ho and his colleagues greatly improved the lives of countless patients and prevented many more new infections.

Ho has continued working as an HIV researcher, dedicating almost his entire professional career to finding a cure. His tireless work and amazing determination make him one of medicine's greatest heroes, and his work has saved lives all over the world.

◆ **EDDIE LODEWIJK VAN HALEN** was one of the greatest **rock guitarists** of all time. During his career, he played to audiences around the globe in amazing, energetic performances.

Born on January 26, 1955, in Amsterdam, Netherlands, Eddie and his family immigrated to the United States when he was a young boy and settled in Pasadena, California. As a child, Eddie was enrolled in classical piano lessons. Even from a young age, Eddie had a natural love for music, and he quickly became a talented musician. When he was a teenager, however, Eddie switched from playing classical music to playing rock. While Eddie began playing the guitar, his brother learned how to play the drums. Together, they formed their very first band called Mammoth.

In 1974, when Eddie was only nineteen years old, the two brothers met singer David Lee Roth and bassist Michael Anthony. They invited both musicians to join their band, and soon Mammoth become a popular rock band in Los Angeles, California. In 1977, only three years later, Eddie and Mammoth were discovered by rock legend Gene Simmons of the band KISS. This meeting helped launch Eddie into a new world of fame and success. One year later, Eddie and the newly renamed band, Van Halen, signed with Warner Bros and began releasing records.

Van Halen was an immediate success, and rock fans everywhere fell in love with Eddie's unique, masterful style of guitar playing. Van Halen's very first record went platinum only half a year after it was released. Throughout the 1970s, 1980s, and 1990s, Eddie became one of the most famous and beloved rock guitarists of all time. Van Halen worked extremely hard to make music and released more than a dozen albums.

Although the members of the band changed over time, Eddie and his skill helped keep Van Halen one of the best rock bands through the ages. Eddie continued to produce amazing music and sell millions of records. He also earned an impressive number of awards and honors, and many of his albums with Van Halen helped shape the rock 'n' roll genre into what it is today. In 2007, the band was inducted into the **Rock and Roll Hall of Fame**.

Although Eddie passed away in 2020, his legacy lives on in the thousands of fans he inspired, and his music remains some of the best rock of all time.

◆ **IMAN ABDULMAJID,** a Somalian American woman, became known as one of the most famous **supermodels** of the late twentieth century, in addition to her successful work as an **entrepreneur** and **activist**.

Iman Abdulmajid was born on July 25, 1955, in Mogadishu, Somalia, to a wealthy family. Her father was a Somalian ambassador, and her mother was a respected doctor. Throughout her childhood, Iman lived in many places. When she was four, she moved to Egypt to attend boarding school. After returning to Somalia for some time, she also moved with her family to Kenya. In Kenya, Iman studied political science at the University of Nairobi.

While in Nairobi, Abdulmajid's modeling career began when she was eighteen. While walking down the street one day, she was noticed by a famous photographer named Peter Beard, who was struck by her looks. He immediately asked Abdulmajid if she had ever modeled. That day, Beard became the first photographer to work with Abdulmajid, but he would not be the last.

When Beard returned to the United States, his photographs of Abdulmajid quickly became very popular. Four months later, Abdulmajid immigrated to the United States to begin her modeling career in earnest. She was signed to Wilhelmina Models and began to work in high fashion runway shows. Abdulmajid was very beautiful, but much of her success was because she looked so different from most other models at the time. Her unique features redefined the standards of beauty in modern fashion. Because of this, Abdulmajid helped create opportunities for people of different backgrounds to work in fashion.

Abdulmajid was so wildly popular that some fashion designers made entire lines of clothing specifically devoted to her. In the 1990s, she also began her own line of makeup and beauty products. Focused on serving women of all skin tones, Abdulmajid's products were a massive success and helped to change the makeup industry.

During her work as a model, however, Abdulmajid began to dream of doing more. In 1992, she traveled with a film crew to Somalia. She filmed a documentary there to show the world the reality of life in her home country. She documented war, famine, and struggles, but also featured the vibrant and joyful culture of her native land. After this trip, Abdulmajid was inspired to continue her humanitarian work. Since that time, she has continued to hold fundraisers and events to help people all around the world, using her fame and influence to help the less fortunate.

◆ **Cello player, composer**, and **performer YO-YO MA** is recognized today as one of the greatest musicians in the world and one of the greatest cello players of all time.

Born on October 7, 1955, in Paris, France, Yo-Yo Ma was the son of Chinese parents who were also musicians. His father, Hiao-Tsiun Ma, was a well-respected violin player and his mother, Marina Lu, was a skilled opera singer. Because of the support of his family and his natural talent, Ma was widely recognized as a musical prodigy. He gave his first cello performance when he was only five years old in France.

Two years later, when Ma was seven, he and his family immigrated to the United States. They made a new home in New York City and began their new life. In New York, Ma continued to study music, and his skill on the cello continued to grow. In 1963, Ma and his sister were both invited to play at an event in Washington, DC. After the event, famous musician Isaac Stern personally suggested that Ma's parents enroll him at Juilliard School, one of the world's most prestigious music schools.

Ma graduated high school at age fifteen, and attended both Harvard—where he earned his bachelor's degree and later an honorary doctorate—and Juilliard, where he continued studying music. From there, Ma's career began in earnest. As he trained, he steadily became one of the most promising young classical musicians in the entire world.

Interestingly, although Ma was such a successful and skilled cellist, he would often skip practices with his teachers. This changed when he met world-renowned cellist Mstislav Rostropovich. Unlike Ma's previous teachers, who had treated him gently because of his natural talent, Rostropovich refused to take it easy on the young Ma.

As his mentor, Rostropovich pushed Ma to greater heights than ever before. His time with Rostropovich changed him, and for the rest of his career, he poured more attention and focus into his music.

As an adult, Ma played and performed on some of the most famous stages all around the world. Fascinated by his unique talent, other musicians and bands traveled to meet and collaborate with him on all different genres of music. From classical to jazz to pop, Ma could play almost any type of music like a natural.

Ma has received hundreds of awards, including the Presidential Medal of Freedom, a Kennedy Center Honor, and a Praemium Imperiale distinction. He is widely considered one of the most talented and accomplished musicians alive. He has influenced music in a way that only the greatest ever have, and his work has inspired thousands to begin playing.

PRAMILA JAYAPAL, an Indian American **writer**, **entrepreneur**, and **politician**, has broken down many boundaries in her life. As the first Indian American woman elected to the U.S. House of Representatives, she inspires people across America to believe that they can achieve their dreams.

Born on September 21, 1965, in Chennai, India, Pramila lived in Indonesia and Singapore for most of her childhood. When she was sixteen years old, however, she immigrated to the United States to begin her college education. Although still very young, Jayapal earned her bachelor's degree from Georgetown University and then her master's degree in business from Northwestern University. While at college, Jayapal was an excellent student and earned very high grades. This helped her after she graduated, and she was almost immediately offered a job by the finance company PaineWebber.

At her new job, Jayapal worked on projects for companies worldwide. She quickly became a very successful and well-respected financial analyst. Despite this, Jayapal felt that she could be doing more with her life, and she soon began her work as a humanitarian. After the September 11 terrorist attacks on the World Trade Center in 2001, Jayapal created an organization called Hate Free Zone to help immigrants who had come to America in hopes of building a better life, just like she had.

Jayapal discovered that she was as talented at humanitarian work as she had been at finance, and she continued helping people all over. Throughout her life, Pramila has fought for the civil rights of women, immigrants, and anyone who needed her protection. Because of Jayapal and the organizations she has founded, America is a stronger, safer place today.

In 2016, Jayapal's work was recognized when she ran for office in Washington state. After a long, hard campaign with very strong competition, Jayapal won the vote and was elected to the U.S. House of Representatives. As a politician, Jayapal has continued the work she began as a private citizen. In government, she consistently fights for those who need help the most and refuses to sacrifice her beliefs.

To date, Jayapal has held many leadership positions in the Democratic Party and has sponsored many bills to help her constituents. She continues to push herself and everyone around her to do better. Pramila Jayapal is a shining example of what can be done with hard work, determination, and a dream.

ANOUSHEH ANSARI is an Iranian American **business leader**, **engineer**, and **entrepreneur** who made history as the first Iranian and the first Muslim woman to have ever traveled into space.

Born on September 12, 1966, in Mashhad, Iran, Anousheh's family worked hard to provide her with as many opportunities as they could. Though she grew up very poor, Anousheh was inspired by her family to work hard and reach for the stars. Her grandmother was a strong role model, and even when the family was struggling, she would encourage Anousheh to study hard and never settle for less than the best.

Because of this, Ansari worked hard in school and quickly demonstrated that she was an excellent student. She learned many languages and showed a particular knack for both math and science. In 1978, Ansari's life was made much harder when the Islamic Revolution began in Iran. During the revolution, her neighborhood became a dangerous place to live. The violence of the revolution continued for more than a year, and when it ended, there was even more danger because Iran went to war with neighboring Iraq. Soon, Ansari and her family realized that she could not achieve her dreams if they remained in the country. Because of this, she immigrated with her sister and mother to the United States when she was seventeen years old. This began a new chapter in Ansari's life, and she worked harder than ever before.

After graduating from high school, Ansari enrolled at George Mason University where she studied computer engineering and electronics. Even while taking classes, she worked multiple jobs to support herself and her family. Despite this, Ansari earned excellent grades and graduated from university with honors. Soon after graduation, she was offered a job with a company called MCI Communications, and she worked there while also earning her master's degree.

In 1993, Ansari and her husband began a company named Telecom Technologies, which gave engineering advice to other companies. Through a mixture of hard work and creativity, Telecom Technologies eventually became very successful. Ansari's ambitions were even greater than one company, though, and she continued to push herself higher and higher.

In 2006, Ansari was offered a spot on a flight into space with a company called Space Adventures. She spent six months learning how to be an astronaut, and then, only one week before she turned forty years old, Ansari became the first woman, Iranian, and Muslim to travel into space as a civilian.

The experience changed Ansari. When she returned to Earth, she began to invest in space travel. Today, Ansari uses her skills and company to help push humanity toward understanding the stars, and she hopes that, one day, every person will have the chance to go to space, too.

JERRY YANG, a Taiwanese American **business leader** and **entrepreneur** became one of the most successful people in America through smart business moves, constant innovation, and hard work.

Born Chih-Yuan Yang on November 6, 1968, in Taipei, Taiwan, Jerry was raised almost entirely by his mother after his father passed away when Jerry was only two years old. When Jerry was ten, he and his family immigrated to America where his mother taught English to other immigrants. Because of this, Jerry learned English very quickly. Although he spoke none before his family had left Taiwan, he completely mastered the language in just three years.

After finishing high school in San Jose, California, Yang enrolled in classes at Stanford University. There, he studied science and earned both a bachelor's degree and master's degree in electrical engineering in only four years. While at Stanford, Yang met David Filo, who would go on to become one of Yang's good friends and business partners.

Following his graduation from Stanford, Yang set out to begin his career. Instead of working for other people, though, he decided to build his own company. Together with David, Yang began researching ways that he could improve the internet. Eventually, the pair developed and launched a website called Yahoo.com. Yahoo helped people on the internet search for information and discover almost anything they wanted. It was a massive success. One of the very first **search engines**, Yahoo would go on to become part of Yang's multi-billion-dollar company, Yahoo! Inc.

For more than ten years, Yang led the company, amassing a fortune and helping revolutionize the way people used the internet. During this time, he also led other companies, using his keen intellect and strong business skills to build several strong ventures. In 2012, Yang decided to leave Yahoo! for good, when he shifted his focus to helping young inventors and businesspeople begin their careers.

Specifically, Yang cofounded AME Cloud Ventures to invest in startup technology companies that he though had strong ideas. He did this to help shape modern technology and share his experience with the next generation of rising entrepreneurs.

Despite the stacked odds and personal hardship, Jerry Yang's hard work, creativity, and commitment to the world of computer technology helped him become one of America's most successful businesspeople. Even today, he continues to play a huge role in revolutionizing the internet and how we use it.

Indian American actor and **film director M. NIGHT SHYAMALAN** is known for producing some of the most popular and daring contemporary films. His unique twisty and unpredictable thriller style has earned him many fans around the world.

Born Manoj Nelliyattu Shyamalan on August 6, 1970, in the town of Mahé, India, to a wealthy family, both of Shyamalan's parents were skilled and well-respected doctors. Only six weeks after he was born, Shyamalan's family immigrated to the United States. There, they settled in Penn Valley, Pennsylvania, where Shyamalan would grow up. Although he was raised Hindu, he attended classes at Catholic and Episcopal schools in the area. This experience made Shyamalan feel very lonely as a child, and he focused intensely on his schoolwork.

Although his parents hoped that he would follow in their footsteps and study medicine, the young Shyamalan had a natural fascination with movies and how they were made. During his childhood, he made almost fifty amateur movies using a camera he was given as a present. Even though he did not want to study medicine, Shyamalan was still an excellent student and earned very good grades. Because of this, he was awarded a scholarship to New York University (NYU) Tisch School of the Arts. In New York City, Shyamalan studied filmmaking and other media art.

While still an undergrad, Shyamalan directed and produced his first real film titled *Praying with Anger*, which was loosely based on his own life. Although his first two films did not perform well in theaters, Shyamalan became an overnight star after his third film, *The Sixth Sense*, was released in 1999. A scary thriller that kept viewers on their toes, the movie earned Shyamalan a huge following of devoted fans. *The Sixth Sense* was the most popular movie that year, and it earned Shyamalan seven Oscar nominations. The film firmly cemented his reputation as a talented young director.

In the 2000s, Shyamalan continued to make movies and develop his style; many of his movies were in the supernatural thriller genre and featured shocking twist endings. Movies such as *Unbreakable*, *The Village*, and *Signs* have all established Shyamalan as one of the best directors of his genre and of our time.

ELON MUSK is a **business leader**, **scientist**, and **entrepreneur** whose businesses and investments have made him one of the wealthiest people in the history of the world. A unique man with his own style and personality, he has played a major role in shaping the twenty-first century and its technology.

Born on June 28, 1971, in Pretoria, South Africa, Elon's family was very wealthy. Because of this, he was afforded many opportunities and the best schooling available. Elon was naturally curious about technology and had a very sharp intellect as a child. He also loved to read books.

In 1989, Musk enrolled in Queen's University in Canada. Two years later, he transferred to the University of Pennsylvania, Philadelphia. He took courses in both economics and physics, and graduated with bachelor's degrees in both subjects.

Musk continued his graduate education at Stanford University, where he had planned to study advanced energy physics. After only two days on campus, though, Musk decided to drop out to become an entrepreneur. Fascinated by the power and potential of the internet, Musk created a company named Zip2 in 1995. This company created guides to help people navigate through different cities and was used by websites for both the *New York Times* and *Chicago Tribune*. Musk's decision to become an entrepreneur literally paid off when he sold Zip2 for almost $350 million four years later.

Not ready to retire with his fortune while still so young, Musk continued to create wildly successful businesses. The same year that he sold Zip2, Musk and his brother launched X.com, a website designed to help people make payments online. This company would eventually be renamed to PayPal, which would grow into one of the largest money-transferring websites of its kind.

In 2002, Elon Musk officially became a billionaire when he sold PayPal for $1.5 billion. With this fortune, he again went on to create a new company. This time, however, Musk decided to try a new type of business entirely.

Named SpaceX, Elon Musk's third company was focused on building advanced spacecrafts to use for commercial trips into space, much like how airplanes are used by the average traveler today. Although a huge risk, the decision proved brilliant for Musk. In 2008, NASA hired Elon Musk and SpaceX to begin bringing supplies to the International Space Station (ISS). This gave the company a huge boost and helped make it the most successful privately owned space business ever.

In addition to Space X, Musk also kept a few other ventures viable. He helped found **Tesla**, an electric car company, and took over as CEO in 2008. He also played a role in starting a nonprofit that promotes artificial intelligence research, a neurotechnology company, and a tunnel construction company.

Currently the richest man in the world—and with an incredible story and diverse business portfolio—many believe that there is still much more to come from Elon Musk.

- A Russian American **entrepreneur, developer**, and **computer scientist, SERGEY BRIN** cocreated Google and changed the landscape of the internet permanently.

Born on August 21, 1973, in Moscow, Russia, Sergey Brin and his family left their home country to escape the discrimination and anti-Semitism in Russia. The Brin family lived in both Vienna, Austria, and Paris, France, for short periods before finally immigrating to the United States in 1979. In America, Sergey's father Mikhail worked as a mathematics professor at the University of Maryland, and the family settled into their new home.

Although Sergey was a bright and attentive student in primary school, his father took special care to tutor him as well. At home, Sergey learned mathematics far beyond what was being taught at his age in public school.

In 1990, after Sergey graduated from high school, he enrolled at the University of Maryland, and after three years, he graduated with a bachelor's degree in computer science at only nineteen years old. Continuing on, Brin began classes at Stanford University, where he met a friend and future business partner, Larry Page. The two had much in common, and both had advanced expertise in computer science. Throughout their graduate school years, the two friends researched the internet and ways to improve it.

After Brin graduated with his doctorate from Stanford, he and Page developed a search engine that they named Google, after a term used in mathematics. With a $1 million starting investment—which they had borrowed from friends and family—the two officially launched Google in 1998. Over the next several years, the company grew steadily as the internet became more sophisticated. In 2004, after Google had become one of the busiest search engines in the world, the company began selling stocks. Overnight, both Brin and Page became billionaires.

Although Brin could have easily retired, he chose instead to continue working, hoping to solve new problems and become more successful. In 2006, Google bought the video-sharing platform YouTube to diversity its business. Brin continues to work as director of the company that runs both Google and YouTube, using his impressive experience and talent to continue their growth.

ILHAN OMAR is a Somalian American **activist** and **politician** who has overcome incredibly overwhelming odds and hardship to become a true American success story. After becoming one of the best-known and most outspoken junior members of Congress, Omar represents a new generation of American politicians.

Born on October 4, 1982, in Mogadishu, Somalia, Ilhan's early life was marked by personal tragedy and challenges. When Ilhan was only two years old, her mother passed away, and she was raised by her father and other relatives. Although her family loved her very much and was supportive, Ilhan faced even more challenges when civil war broke out. At eight years old, she and her family fled their home to a refugee camp in Kenya where they lived in limbo for four years. In 1995, Ilhan and her family finally immigrated to the United States after being given asylum as refugees.

Omar and her family settled in Virginia, where they made their new home. For the first few years of her time in America, she studied hard to learn the English language, using television shows to help. Although she was a very bright and hard-working student, she was often bullied in school because of where she was born.

In 1997, Omar's family moved again, this time to Minneapolis, Minnesota. There was a large population of Somali immigrants in the area, which helped Omar feel more comfortable. After graduating from high school, she enrolled in classes at North Dakota State University where she learned about political science and international studies. After earning a bachelor's degree, Omar began educating communities in Minnesota about food and nutrition. As a young woman, she was inspired by her grandfather to help communities around her and to eventually work in politics.

As a young professional, Omar increasingly worked more and more in politics. She earned a reputation as a tough but kind woman who genuinely wanted to help the people around her. In 2016, after a tough election against another Somalian American candidate, Omar won the race for the Minnesota House of Representatives. With her win, Ilhan officially became the first Somali American person to hold such a position in the history of the United States.

After a few years in the state legislature, she set her sights even higher. In 2018, Omar ran for a seat in the **U.S. House of Representatives**—and she won with an overwhelming 78 percent of the vote! With this election, she again made history as the first Somali American elected to the U.S. Congress, and as one of the first two Muslim women elected in history. Omar's victory even prompted the House of Representatives to modify its standing ban on head coverings, making her the first woman to wear a **hijab** on the House floor.

Omar's amazing story and her commitment to speaking up for her constituents quickly made her one of the most well-known politicians in the country. She set an example of using her position to fight fiercely for fairness and justice, and she still refuses to sacrifice her beliefs.

TRIVIA QUESTIONS

1. What type of animal is John James Audubon known for studying? What is the purpose of the Audubon Society? (See no. 3)

2. To which charitable causes did Andrew Carnegie donate a significant amount of money? (See no. 8)

3. What were the first words Alexander Graham Bell successfully spoke through his transmitter? (See no. 10)

4. Who was the first U.S. citizen to be canonized by the Roman Catholic Church? (See no. 15)

5. For which automobile companies did William Knudsen work? (See no. 19)

6. Why did Emmy Noether leave her home country of Germany for the United States? (See no. 22)

7. Who is recognized as the third best-selling poet in history? What was the name of his most successful book? (See no. 25)

8. Name a few of the buildings that Ludwig Mies van der Rohe famously designed. (See no. 28)

9. What disease was the "Cori cycle" instrumental in treating? (See no. 35)

10. What actions did Mabel Ping-Hua Lee take to fight for women's suffrage? (See no. 39)

11. What was the name of the top-secret project on which Edward Teller worked? What was the purpose of the project? (See no. 53)

12. What did Joyce Chen introduce to mainstream American life? (See no. 62)

13. What genre was Isaac Asimov known for writing? (See no. 63)

14. Who created the "five stages of grief" concept? What are the five stages? (See no. 67)

15. What career in music did Seiji Ozawa find after becoming unable to continue his piano performance career? (See no. 72)

16. What computer programming language did Bjarne Stroustrup help create? (See no. 88)

17. What major website did Jerry Yang help create? What did it do? (See no. 96)

18. Ilhan Omar's election to the U.S. House of Representatives marked her as the "first" in several respects—what are they? (See no. 100)

PROJECT SUGGESTIONS

1. Choose one of the people from this book and write a one-page fictional diary entry for one day in that person's life. Pick a day that had some significance for the individual—a day when they achieved some long-held dream or goal, or the day they won a major award or received some official recognition. Alternatively, choose a day on which the person faced a severe setback or was frustrated in some way by a lack of success. Describe the person's thoughts and feelings with as much detail as you can.

2. Arrange a "meeting" of two people in this book who could never have met in real life. Choose individuals from different eras, either from similar professions or walks of life or from completely different ones. Imagine what their meeting would be like. Write one to two pages describing the scenario of their encounter and create a dialogue. What kinds of questions do you think they would ask each other? Would one be surprised about the things the other had done in their lifetime? Be as imaginative as you can.

INDEX

OUT NOW:

100 African Americans Who Shaped American History

100 American Women Who Shaped American History

100 Americans Who Shaped American History

100 Artists Who Shaped World History

100 Athletes Who Shaped Sports History

100 Authors Who Shaped World History

100 Baseball Legends Who Shaped Sports History

100 Battles That Shaped World History

100 Books That Shaped World History

100 Colonial Leaders Who Shaped World History

100 Disasters That Shaped World History

100 Events That Shaped World History

100 Explorers Who Shaped World History

100 Families Who Shaped World History

100 Folk Heroes Who Shaped World History

100 Great Cities of World History

100 Hispanic and Latino Americans Who Shaped American History

100 Inventions That Shaped World History

100 Medical Milestones That Shaped World History

100 Men Who Shaped World History

100 Military Leaders Who Shaped World History

100 Native Americans Who Shaped American History

100 Natural Wonders of the World

100 Relationships That Shaped World History

100 Scientists Who Shaped World History

100 Ships and Planes That Shaped World History

100 Spiritual Leaders Who Shaped World History

100 Wars That Shaped World History

100 Women Who Shaped World History

100 World Leaders Who Shaped World History